JAPANESE KITCHEN KNIVES

JAPANESE

KODANSHA USA

KITCHEN KNIVES

Essential Techniques and Recipes

Hiromitsu Nozaki

with Kate Klippensteen

PHOTOGRAPHS BY Yasuo Konishi

C O N T E N T S

Published by Kodansha USA, Inc.
451 Park Avenue South
New York, NY 10016

Distributed in the United Kingdom and continental Europe
by Kodansha Europe Ltd.

Copyright © 2009, 2012 by Hiromitsu Nozaki, Kate Klippensteen.
Photographs copyright © 2009, 2012 by Yasuo Konishi.
All rights reserved. Printed in South Korea.
ISBN: 978-156836-490-2

First edition published in Japan in 2009 by Kodansha International
First US edition 2012 by Kodansha USA

22 21 20 19   5 4

The Library of Congress has cataloged the earlier printing as follows:

Library of Congress Cataloging-in-Publication Data

Nozaki, Hiromitsu.
  Japanese kitchen knives : essential techniques and recipes
/ Hiromitsu Nozaki with Kate Klippensteen ; photographs by
Yasuo Konishi.
    p. cm.
  Includes bibliographical references and index.
  ISBN 978-4-7700-3076-4 (alk. paper)
  1. Knives--Japan. 2. Cookery, Japanese. I. Klippensteen,
Kate, 1963- II. Title.
  TX657.K54N693 2009
  641.5952--dc22
                          2009000117

www.kodanshausa.com

THE DEBA

THE YANAGIBA

F O R E W O R D

A kitchen knife is a simple tool to cut food, which makes it easier to lift—with chopsticks or a fork—and easier to eat. Yet there is another important reason to use a knife on ingredients, and that is to improve flavor.

Take a tomato, for example, and the act of slicing. A knife with a dull edge will not immediately pierce the skin. It can saw through the tomato, which in essence is actually crushing the flesh. And while the slice might look fine at a glance, closer inspection will reveal an ill-defined edge and a dull surface. A knife with a sharp blade, however, cuts through the fiber in a single clean stroke. The cut edge will be sharp and the surface of the tomato will be as smooth and shiny as a mirror. It's clear to the eye which slice looks tastier.

And you will be surprised by how much better food tastes if it's cut with a sharp Japanese kitchen knife, called a *hocho*. A tomato cut with a dull knife loses juice and *umami* elements, and even when eaten immediately, the texture is limp. A slice of tomato cut with a sharp knife, however, will overwhelm you with its natural juiciness and umami.

The same goes for sashimi. A knife slices through the fish's fiber, so—just as in slicing tomatoes—applying minimum pressure on the flesh is imperative. Pushing or sawing the blade though the elastic flesh of the fish should be avoided, which is why a long, thin, single-ground blade, such as the *yanagiba* knife—that needless to say, is always kept sharp—is ideal.

A yanagiba is pulled through the sashimi; the blade is drawn through the fillets in an arcing motion, from the heel to the tip. While a double-ground knife, angled on both sides, parts the flesh evenly on both sides like a wedge, a single-ground knife applies pressure only on one side. Since only minimum pressure has been applied to the fish fiber, the sashimi slices have a wonderfully sharp edge and glossy surface.

There are several factors that give traditionally forged Japanese knives their extreme sharpness. Their single-ground construction is one reason, but the techniques used in forging are also vital. These knives are not cut from a steel sheet, but are made from chunks of molten steel, hammered many times until they take shape. The repeated heating and hammering, along with annealing, quenching, and cooling, make the steel hard, yet elastic, and give it the strength to hold an edge. If the temperature of the hearth isn't right, or if the knife is not heated enough or is overheated, or if any other variable is incorrect, the finished tool will lack that hardness and elasticity, and will be prone to cracking and chipping. Forging requires a precise technique that can only be accomplished by a skilled and dedicated artisan.

The knives I use are made in Sakai, a city near Osaka that is a traditional center for handmade knives and other cutting tools. Many knife companies elsewhere have mechanized certain parts of the knife-making process. In Sakai, however, the separate tasks involved in making a knife, including forging, sharpening and attaching the wood handles, are divided among artisans. Each division has an old artisan, or a few young persons training to become expert in that task, and all the divisions work together over the several days it takes to make a knife.

If you are lucky enough to own an expertly forged knife from Sakai or one of the other artisan towns, please don't store it away. A kitchen knife is a functional tool, not an art object. Don't hoard it, but use it, and do your best not to let it rust. The best way to display such a knife is through everyday use in your kitchen.

A Japanese knife may be forged in one of two ways. *Honyaki*, traditionally forged knives, are made entirely of high-carbon steel using a process similar to the one used to forge Japanese swords.

Knives forged using the *awase* method are made of two materials, high-carbon steel and soft iron. The first forms a hard cutting edge and the iron a strong spine and tang resistant to chipping and cracking. The repeated heating and pounding process (above) helps to drive out impurities from the metal while merging the two materials. During the process, the temperature of the hearth reaches 1400°C (2550°F).

After basic shaping by further pounding, the knife is coated with clay to stabilize the temperature and facilitate annealing (right), which hardens the steel.

After another round of heating, the awase blade is quenched in water (left) to further harden the metal. It is then reheated as part of a tempering process that gives the steel resilience and keeps it from becoming too brittle. The forged blade is then passed to the edge crafter for further shaping and precise sharpening.

A knife-crafter's workshop in Sakai (right) is dimly lit on purpose: the craftsman needs to clearly see the color of the steel as it is heated in order to gauge the temperature correctly.

The knife is truly the foundation of Japanese cuisine, and the act of cutting is fundamental. An oft-used maxim in Japanese cooking, "*katsu-shu-ho-ju*" (often shortened to *kappo*), literally means "Cut first, then simmer," stressing the belief that "to cut" is actually "to cook." From ancient times, Japanese cuisine has had a strong focus on cutting techniques, which extends beyond cutting raw foods such as sashimi and salad greens to make them look attractive on the plate. Even food items that might be simmered—and therefore might not be prominently visible later—must be cut artistically at the preparation stage. Potatoes, carrots, onions and other vegetables all must be shaped with precision and beauty. There is a strong aesthetic tradition in Japan that links the appearance of food to good flavor.

Yet the act of cutting is, in fact, very simple. If you own a very sharp knife, you are basically sharing the same conditions that exist in a professional kitchen. What makes the gap in the level of technique between the professional and the home cook is a deep knowledge, mastered through long practice, of knife fundamentals, the attributes of food, and the science of cooking.

After forging, the still dull blade is given to another master to create the ridge line and cutting edge. This consists of about thirty steps of sharpening, polishing, and correcting distortions in the blade (left). The process transforms dull blades, such as the ones next to the wood block in the photo at right, into cutting tools. In Sakai, the finished blade is then sent to another master, who attaches the handle (made of ebony or *honoki* or other woods that have been ordered by the retailer) and water buffalo-horn collar. Natural plant oils are then rubbed on the blade to prevent rusting (right) before the knife is packed for delivery.

This book covers the three major single-ground knives—the *usuba*, *deba*, and *yanagiba*. I have tried to fully explain the structure and purpose of Japanese knives, as well as different techniques that can be applied in their use, in the hopes that it will help give readers a clear understanding of blade direction and cutting angle. For this reason, the process cuts have been photographed from the chef's perspective. (This differs from most practical knife books, which photograph the process from the angle of the viewer.)

Don't be afraid to experiment. If the fish in the deba section are unfamiliar, go out and search for fresh local species that are similar. If practicing the rotary peeling technique on a hard *daikon* radish is difficult, why not switch to a softer zucchini to start?

The most important thing I hope readers of this book will discover is that the act of cutting with the exquisitely sharp edge of a single-ground, hand-forged knife is truly enjoyable, even thrilling. No one who has ever felt this thrill could go back to the tedium and frustration of cutting with a dull knife. I firmly believe that with a good knife, cooking will become a truly heightened experience.

Hiromitsu Nozaki
Tokyo, 2009

GETTING STARTED

CUTTING POSTURE *

For both beginners and professionals, basic posture and positioning are crucial. Maintaining the correct stance allows the knife to be wielded with minimal force and effort; it also allows a clear view of the board and surroundings.

To assume the proper stance, face the cutting board and stand firmly, legs about shoulder-width apart. A distance of about two fists should separate the body and the cutting board. Next, slide the right foot a half-step back and turn it out about 45 degrees. This frees the right arm and knife hand, allowing them to move straight up and down without any interference.

Keep the upper right arm against the ribcage, closing the armpit. As the right foot is back and turned outward, this position naturally forms a kind of bulwark. In this position the right arm extends straight to the cutting board. With the left shoulder and hip bent slightly forward, the left side of the body curves round to meet the right hand, and the left arm should form a half circle. With the eyes focused on the knife, the tucked left index and middle fingers should rest against the back of the knife. To

*All the directions in this book are for use with right-handed knives. Left-handed knives can be specially ordered by left-handed readers, who should simply reverse the directions.

cut vegetables *katsuramuki* style (rotary peeling, page 26), lift both the knife and the hand holding the vegetable to work at chest level.

Filleting fish with the *deba* knife may require the body to shift as the knife moves, depending on the size of the fish. But the basic posture is important; that is, standing at an angle to the cutting board with the knife in the back hand.

To use the *yanagiba* knife, which has a longer blade, it may be necessary to stand a little further from the cutting board. In any case, making the left side into a solid bulwark is very important when using the yanagiba; this will make it easy to cut sashimi as cleanly and precisely as possible.

KNIFE ANATOMY

To use this book efficiently, familiarity with the terms used for the various parts of the knife is essential. English words have been used as much as possible, but some of the terms—*shinogi*, for example—have no English equivalent, so the Japanese word has been used. In reading through the instructions for how to execute various techniques, it may be helpful to refer to this page frequently. Likewise, when learning how to fillet fish in the deba section, it may be useful to refer to the diagram showing the anatomy of a fish on page 150.

The illustrations here show the metal content and distribution of both the single-forged *honyaki* and steel-jacketed *awase* knives. The traditionally-forged honyaki knife is made entirely of *hagane* high-carbon steel, while the awase uses hagane carbon steel for the cutting edge and *jigane* soft iron for the spine and upper blade body.

SECTION VIEW

Steel-jacketed *Awase* (*Kasumi*)   Single-forged *Honyaki*

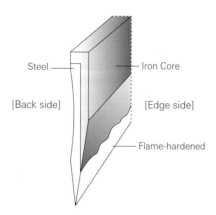

Steel — Iron Core

[Back side]   [Edge side]

Flame-hardened

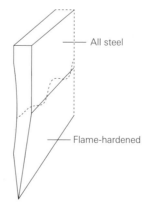

All steel

Flame-hardened

16

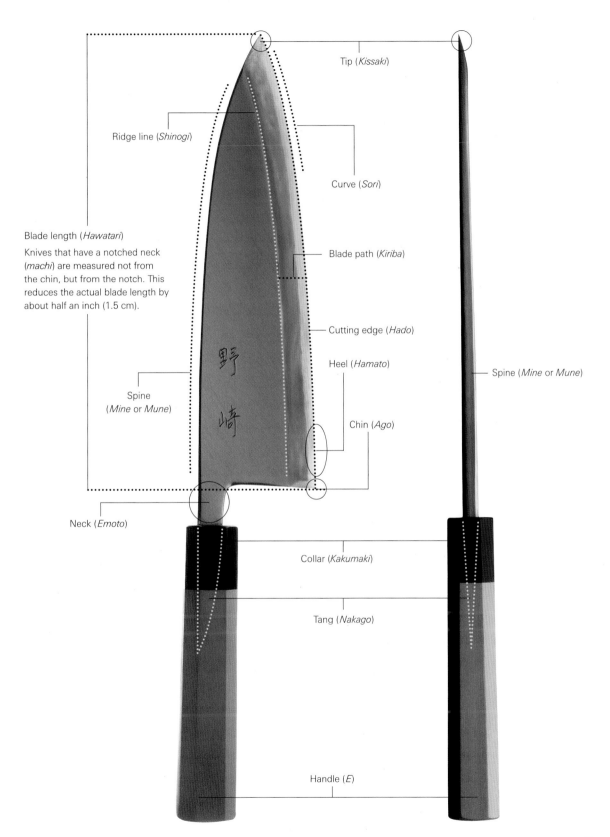

Tip (*Kissaki*)

Ridge line (*Shinogi*)

Curve (*Sori*)

Blade length (*Hawatari*)

Knives that have a notched neck (*machi*) are measured not from the chin, but from the notch. This reduces the actual blade length by about half an inch (1.5 cm).

Blade path (*Kiriba*)

Cutting edge (*Hado*)

Spine
(*Mine* or *Mune*)

Heel (*Hamato*)

Spine (*Mine* or *Mune*)

Chin (*Ago*)

野崎

Neck (*Emoto*)

Collar (*Kakumaki*)

Tang (*Nakago*)

Handle (*E*)

17

KNIFE CONTROL

By adjusting the grip, a knife can be handled in any number of ways, depending on the desired technique and the amount of force needed to cut. Understanding the blade angle of a single-ground edge is equally important. After sufficient practice and use, the knife will feel like an extension of the arm rather than a separate tool.

The standard method of gripping a knife is pictured in photo A, which shows how the usuba is held to cut strips. Holding the knife near the heel and pressing the right index finger against the far side of the blade helps to stabilize the knife.

Photo B shows how to hold the usuba to peel off thin sheets or make decorative cuts with the knife while working at chest level.

When filleting fish with a deba (photo C) or when cutting sashimi by pulling the long yanagiba knife (photo D), the index finger can help to precisely control the blade angle. This extended finger also helps to feel the presence of bones, the border between flesh and skin, and even tender membrane at the tip of the knife.

Using a deba to cut through tough bones often requires extra force. This can be

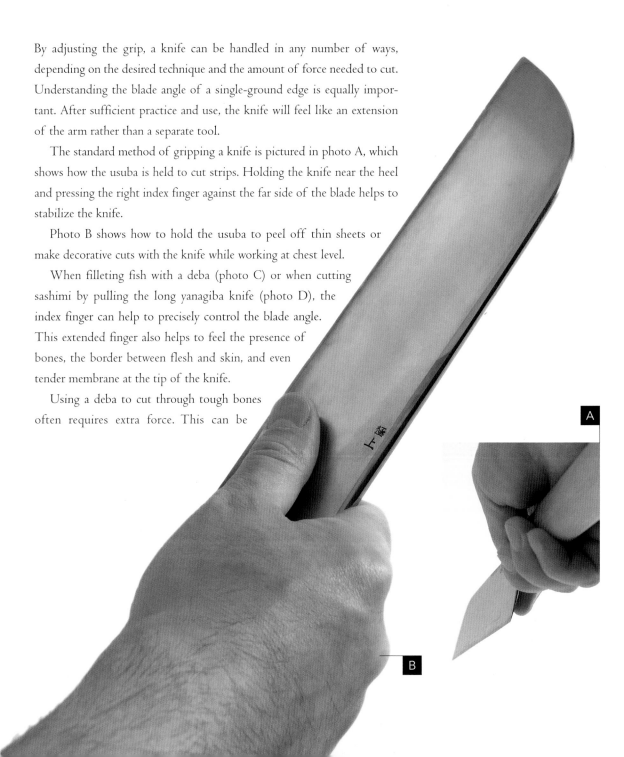

A

B

accomplished by tapping the spine of the knife with the left fist (photo E), or by sliding the grip down the handle (photo F) and using the weight of the knife like a cleaver.

The Three Main Knives

THE USUBA

The *usuba* knife may look humble, but great skill is required to execute the elegant, detailed cutting techniques for which it was designed. Apprentice chefs, for example, spend years practicing with this knife to peel a daikon radish into a continuous transparent sheet in order to perfect their *katsuramuki* rotary peeling technique.

The usuba is designed for cutting vegetables, and its principal features are specifically tailored to this purpose. Like the *deba* and *yanagiba*, the usuba blade is single-ground; that is, sharpened only on one side. Compared to other knives, however, the blade of the usuba is very thin and broad; the word "usuba" translates, in fact, to "thin cutting edge." This allows for

extremely delicate cutting techniques, such as katsuramuki and *kazari-giri* decorative cutting, as well as paper-thin vertical slicing (of ginger or garlic, for example). The fine blade and slender spine of the usuba also minimize the crushing of the vegetables' fibers as they are cut. The usuba slices cleanly through the fibers, leaving a sharp, shiny surface on the cut side.

Each section of the usuba blade is used for a specific purpose: the central part is used for *ken* needle cutting and general peeling, such as katsuramuki peeling; the heel of the blade is good for beveling. The upper part of the blade and the pointed tip are used for precision work like kazari-giri decorative carving. The breadth of the usuba blade facilitates cut-

Usuba, *higashigata* (Kanto-style), 8.4 inches (210 mm). Honyaki, *shirogami* steel, with white water buffalo-horn collar and *honoki* wood handle. (Tsukiji Masamoto)

ting through large vegetables like cabbage without the slices scattering apart as they are shredded, and it also makes it possible to peel vegetables in long, wide strips. Most importantly, the cutting edge of the usuba is completely straight, so it ends up flush against the surface of the board when slicing.

Unlike slicing with a Western knife, where the point is used as a pivot—and the edge goes from diagonal to horizontal through the course of the cut—the usuba blade is kept parallel to the board throughout the cut. With the usuba, slicing is accomplished with a motion called *utsu* in Japanese: moving the knife slightly toward the far side of the board while cutting straight down. The weight of the blade accomplishes most of the cut, while the slight movement to the far side of the board does the rest. Professionals prefer to use a slightly heavier usuba for greater efficiency.

Usuba knives may be forged using either the *honyaki* or *awase* methods, and are shaped in one of two main styles. The *higashigata*, developed in the Kanto area (around Tokyo), resembles a cleaver with its rectangular profile and squared-off corners. The *kamagata* usuba, which was developed in the Kansai area of Western Japan, has a rounded profile—the front of the blade is not square, like the higashigata, but curves gently down toward the tip. Because it has a more open pointed tip, the kamagata is better suited to detailed tasks like kazari-giri decorative cutting. Both styles of usuba have a completely straight cutting edge. Whether using a higashigata or kamagata usuba, professional chefs generally select blades between 8 and 10 inches (21–24 cm) long. For non-professionals, a shorter blade (7–8 inches / 18–21 cm long) is easier to handle.

The usuba's development is directly related to the important role played by vegetables in Japanese cuisine. Along with rice and fish, wild and cultivated vegetables, as well as sea vegetables, form a significant part of the traditional diet. *Shojin ryori*, Japan's distinctive Zen vegetarian cuisine, came into being with the rise of Buddhism in the Muromachi Period. To this day, vegetables are still a principal component of home-cooked meals in Japan, which accounts for the emergence and continued prevalence of usuba knives as tools used exclusively for dealing with them.

Usuba, *kamagata* (Kansai-style), 9.6 inches (240 mm). Awase, *aogami* steel, *suminagashi* pattern with *kokutan* ebony handle and a white water buffalo-horn band. ("Sakai Ichimonji Tadakuni" insignia / Hiyoshimaru)

A number of variations on the usuba have developed as well. The *muki-mono* knife, for instance, is shaped like the *kamagata* but with a slanted tip. This knife, which comes in many sizes, is used for meticulous garnish work. There is also the *kawamuki* (literally, "skin peeling") knife, which is used for paring and beveling tasks. The kawamuki is smaller and shorter than the usuba, with a blade around 3½ inches (9 cm) long and a handle of equal length, and has a rounded kamagata shape.

A widely used variation on the usuba, developed for home use, is the *nakiri* knife. The nakiri is generally double-ground, though there is a single-ground nakiri. Home cooks who rarely do katsuramuki rotary peeling or similarly detailed tasks find the double-ground blade easier to handle. Furthermore, as nakiri knives are generally awase-forged, they are less expensive and easier to maintain than honyaki-forged usuba knives. Like the usuba, the nakiri comes in two shapes, having either a rectangular or rounded-off profile. In most homes, the nakiri is the knife used for basic vegetable cutting, such as slicing onions, splitting cabbages, and dicing carrots.

The *santoku* ("three-purpose") knife must also be mentioned, as it is ubiquitous in Japanese home kitchens. The santoku, like the usuba, has a narrow spine and thin blade, but the tip is curved, like that of a Western chef's knife. It is used for slicing, dicing, and mincing vegetables and meat; it is not substantial enough for the demands of gutting and cleaving, but it can handle boneless or small-boned cuts of meat. The versatility of the santoku makes it popular; the usuba, by comparison, is more specialized.

The usuba is not a particularly fragile knife, but some general guidelines for its care should be observed. Certain foods will react with the usuba's carbon-steel blade. Acidic foods, for example, as well as salty foods like pickles, will stain the blade and dull it prematurely. After cutting tomatoes, garlic, pickles, or sour fruit like lemons or apples, immediately rinse the blade or wipe it with a damp cloth. Additionally, be aware of the limitations of the blade: its thinness makes it unsuitable for cutting through meat or bones, and it should never be used on frozen foods of any kind. The usuba should be sharpened frequently for safety and ease of use, and always be sure it is completely dry before storing it away.

Josei usuba, *higashigata* (Kanto-style), 8.4 inches (210 mm). Awase, aogami steel with black water buffalo-horn collar and *honoki* wood handle (Aritsugu)

Katsuramuki Rotary Peeling

The *katsuramuki* technique is used to cut a cylindrical vegetable into a continuous paper-thin sheet. The *usuba* knife is essential for katsuramuki because of its thin, straight *kiriba* (blade path). Other knives, like the *deba* or *yanagiba*, have a blade that curves toward the tip, making them impractical for katsuramuki.

Beginners often make the mistake of moving or pushing the blade into the vegetable to cut. For katsuramuki, the vegetable should be rotated toward the knife blade with the free hand while making a slight up-and-down movement with the knife. The thumb of the free hand is the key to good katsuramuki technique. The thumb should be kept at right angles to the knife blade (parallel to the top and bottom of the vegetable cylinder) as the vegetable is rotated. The up stroke (bottom to top) is the one that cuts; the down stroke mainly returns the blade to its original position.

Daikon is not the only vegetable that can be cut with the katsuramuki technique. Softer vegetables such as zucchini or cucumber can also be used, taking off a thicker sheet. (Carrots are a challenge, however, given their hardness.) If the sheet turns out to be bumpy, or too thick, simply julienne it, save it for a salad or stir-fry, and start again.

Creating a cylinder

1. Cut a workable length of *daikon* radish (about 4 inches / 10 cm). For beginners, starting with half that length will be much easier.

2. When holding the daikon, the thumb should be parallel to the cut ends.

3. With the *usuba*, make a shallow cut vertical cut along the side of the daikon. Pushing the daikon against the blade to get the knife edge under the peel, turn the blade so that it is nearly flat against the surface, as in photo 3. Rotate the daikon against the blade by pushing the daikon with the thumb of the free hand. This starts the removal of the peel. Keep the knife-hand steady, moving the blade in a small, straight up-and-down (but not side-to-side) motion, while continuing to rotate the daikon. Keep the straight blade parallel to the daikon. The angle of the blade controls the thickness of the layer removed. Peel off a fairly thick layer to make a uniformly cylindrical shape.

4. This peeled cylinder of daikon or carrot serves as the base for many other cuts, such as *wagiri* round slices. It may be difficult to make a uniform cylinder at first, but practice will lead to improvement.

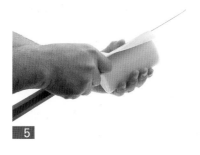

Making paper-thin sheets

5. Holding the usuba at the base of the blade, fold the right index finger behind the knife so it rests against the upper part of the blade. Using the center of the knife blade, begin peeling a thin layer from the cylinder.

6, 7, 8, 9. As you work, rather than pushing the usuba, hold it steady and rotate the daikon against the blade with the thumb of the free hand. (See photos for proper hand position.)

Slide the blade of the usuba in a small up-and-down movement to keep thickness of the sheet uniform. Make sure that the straight edge of the blade stays parallel to the length of the daikon.

To maintain the angle of the usuba, be conscious of the balance of pressure between the right thumb in front of the blade and the index finger behind it. The greater the pressure of the index finger, the thinner the daikon sheet will become. Reducing this pressure will make the sheet thicker.

Continue rotating the daikon against the blade, creating a long, uniformly thin sheet, until only a 1-inch (2.5 cm) cylinder remains.

Katsuramuki-cut daikon is often rolled like a scroll to prevent drying and stored in plastic wrap.

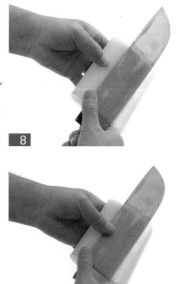

Daikon and Smoked Salmon Rolls

SERVES TWO

Two 4 in. (10 cm) lengths *daikon* radish, cut *katsuramuki*-style into a ¹⁄₁₆ in. (2 mm) thick sheet.

1 piece dried *kombu* kelp, about 2 in. (5 cm) square

2 strips of smoked salmon, ½ in. (1.5 cm) square and 4 in. (10 cm) long

Marinade

1 cup (240 ml) water or *dashi* stock (recipe p. 34)

⅔ cup (160 ml) rice vinegar

⅓ cup (80 ml) mirin

½ tsp. salt

Sauce

3 egg yolks

1 tbsp. rice vinegar

1 tbsp. sugar

Pinch salt

½ tsp. light soy sauce

Place the daikon sheets and kombu in a 1.5% salt water solution (2 cups / 480 ml water and scant 1½ tsp. salt) and soak for 30 minutes until slightly soft. Meanwhile, combine all marinade ingredients in a non-reactive saucepan and bring to a simmer. Cool to room temperature. Remove the daikon sheets from the salt water and pat dry with a cloth or paper towel. Soak in the marinade for an hour.

Roll the sheets of daikon tightly around the smoked salmon. Cut each roll into four rounds. Cover with plastic wrap and set aside.

Bring water to a boil in the lower half of a double-boiler or a medium saucepan. Combine the egg yolks, rice vinegar, sugar, and salt in the top part of the double boiler or a non-reactive, heatproof bowl. Place the egg-yolk mixture over the boiling water, lower the heat to medium and cook gently, stirring continuously with a whisk, until the mixture thickens a little but remains soft.

Arrange the daikon and salmon rounds on a plate and spoon the sauce over.

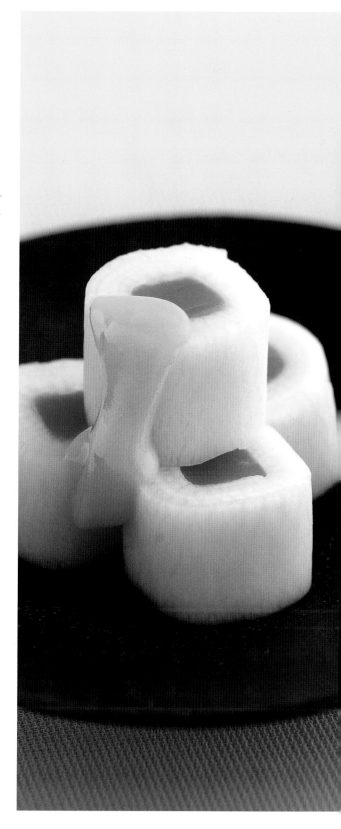

Ken Needle Cut

Sashimi is often served with vegetable garnishes, or *tsuma*, perhaps the most common of which is a heap of shredded *daikon* that serves as a bed for the fish slices. The technique used to shred daikon in this style is called *ken*. As a garnish for sashimi, ken-cut daikon absorbs fishy odors, cleanses the palate and makes an attractive foil for presenting vividly colored sashimi.

Many vegetables, including ginger, potatoes, cucumbers, carrots, garlic, leeks, and red radishes, can also be cut this way. When shredding fibrous vegetables like ginger and daikon, be aware which way the grain of the fiber runs. Slicing in the same direction as the grain will produce stiff, straight needles, while cutting across the grain makes soft threads. In the photo below, the daikon on the left was cut across the grain; the one on the right was cut along the grain.

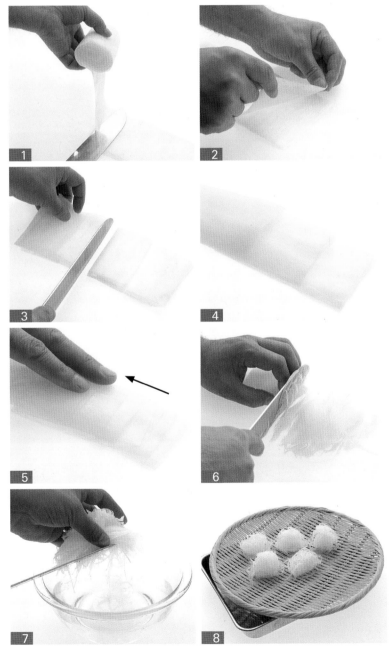

Cutting *daikon* needle strips

1, 2. Peel a 4-inch (10 cm) length of daikon and cut into a paper-thin sheet, katsuramuki style (p. 26). Cut the sheet into squares and stack them up.

3. Cut the stacked sheets at intervals about the width of three fingers.

4, 5. Lay the resulting stacks so that they overlap (photo 4), then gently fan them to the left to make many layers.

To create sharper, stiffer needles, lay the sheets with the grain of the fibers running parallel to the blade. Cut along the grain in very thin strips. If soft threads are desired, lay the sheets so the grain is perpendicular to the blade, then cut across the fibers.

6. When cutting, curl the fingers of the left hand so that the fingertip knuckles press against the blade, controlling the thickness of the strips. Take care to keep the thumb well behind the fingers to avoid getting cut. Cut by smoothly pushing the knife down and away, with the blade held nearly parallel to the cutting board.

7. Place the shredded daikon in a bowl of cold water to crisp.

8. Form ken-cut daikon into heaps for *tsuma* sashimi garnish. The finely sliced needle strips are fluffy and easy to shape into mounds.

Ken-cut zucchini

1. The tender flesh of zucchini makes it easy to cut into sheets. First, cut the zucchini into 2-inch (5 cm) lengths. Use the *katsuramuki* technique (p. 26) to peel the zucchini into a single long ribbon. Because the zucchini is not a uniform cylinder, the ribbon will be narrow at first, becoming more regular in width as you progress. The ribbon should be somewhat thicker than the *daikon* sheet shown in the katsuramuki section.

2. Continue making the ribbon by rotating the zucchini against the blade. Stop when only a small cylindrical core remains.

3. If you are not going to use it immediately, roll the ribbon up like a scroll and enclose it in plastic wrap.

4. Just before serving, cut the ribbon into rectangles and stack them, then fan them sideways. Cut into slivers as described in steps 1 to 8 on p. 31.

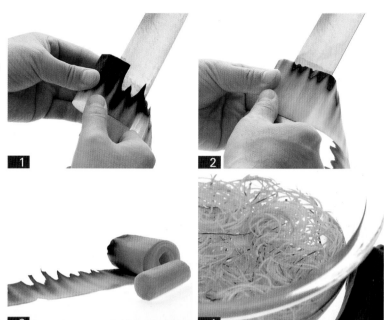

Ken-cut radish

Radishes can be cut into ken needle-strips in the same manner as daikon radish and zucchini. The radish is first peeled *katsuramuki*-style; the sheets are then cut into fine strips. In the first step, the narrow strip of red skin gradually turns into a beautiful red-edged ribbon as it is peeled away. This ribbon can be a beautiful garnish on its own, but the ken-cut strips also make a gorgeous accent on a plate. If the ribbon is placed in ice water before it is cut into strips, the needles will be crisper.

Ken-cut long onion

The mild and versatile Japanese scallion called *naganegi* is often cut into ken-strips. The long white section of the onion has layers much like a leek or green onion. Naganegi is eaten raw, but because it can be tough and fibrous it is often ken-cut, either along or across the grain. Western leeks can also be ken-cut in the same way.

Cut a 3-inch (8 cm) length from the white part of the naganegi. Score almost halfway through and remove the greenish center core (this can be reserved and sliced thinly to sprinkle on top of food). Separate and stack the white layers, and thinly slice them along the grain to make thin strips.

These needle-thin white strips, called *shiraga-negi*, are used as toppings on simmered dishes, as a garnish for sashimi, and as a topping for hot ramen noodles.

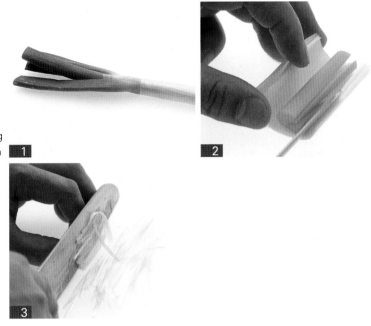

Ken-cut ginger

This technique is used by Japanese chefs to cut *shoga* ginger into extremely thin strips. Ken-cut ginger, also called *hari-shoga* ("hari" means "needle"), can be bundled together for use as a garnish (see "Simmered Eggplant and Chicken Breast" on p. 43). Remove the skin from a knob of ginger, then use the katsuramuki technique to peel the ginger into a thin sheet. The sheet can then be cut along the grain ken-style to form needle strips.

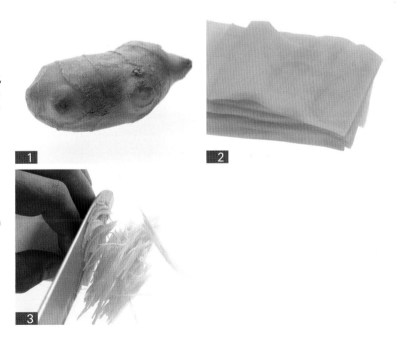

D A S H I

If hand-forged knives are a pillar of Japanese cuisine, *dashi*, the Japanese chef's ubiquitous cooking stock, is another. There are many variations on dashi, from a simple umami-rich broth made only with *kombu* kelp to elaborate versions containing several ingredients. The most common dashi, however, is made with kombu and *katsuobushi*, finely shaved flakes of dried and smoked bonito.

A number of quick and easy dashi options are available, including instant powdered dashi and ready-made dashi-packs—teabag-type sachets that are placed in hot water and simmered with other ingredients. These can be found at many Asian grocery stores. It is best, however, to make dashi from scratch, using high-quality dried kombu and katsuobushi shavings. (In fact, dashi purists insist on shaving their own from the dried block of fish.)

This recipe makes about 2 cups (480 ml) of dashi. Dashi keeps for a day or two if refrigerated; for longer periods, a good trick is to freeze leftover dashi in an ice-cube tray, then place the frozen cubes in a sealed freezer bag to be used as needed. (Ice-cube trays in the U.S. generally hold about ⅛ cup (30 ml) of fluid per cube, but it's best to confirm the volume before using the frozen dashi in a recipe.)

8 in. (20 cm) length dried *kombu* kelp
3 cups (⅓ oz. / 10 g) *katsuobushi* bonito flakes, loosely packed
3 cups (720 ml) water

Lightly wipe the surface of the kombu clean with a damp lint-free cloth. Place the kombu in a medium saucepan, add water and allow to soak for at least 30 minutes. Place the saucepan over medium-low heat. When the liquid comes to a bare simmer (small bubbles form on the sides and bottom of the pan) and the kombu begins to rise to the top, turn off the heat and add the katsuobushi. Let steep uncovered for 1 or 2 minutes until the flakes have sunk to the bottom of the pan. Strain through a sieve lined with cheesecloth. The kombu and katsuobushi can be discarded or used again to make a less refined dashi. Use immediately, refrigerate, or freeze.

Needle-cut Vegetable Salad with Sesame Dressing

Needle-cut vegetables, in addition to being a lovely garnish for sashimi, are great as a salad on their own. This sesame dressing goes well with such a salad.

SERVES FOUR

3 cups (300 g) total *ken* needle-cut vegetables such as *daikon* radish, carrot, ginger, radish and cucumber
1 cup (240 ml) *dashi* stock (recipe above)
¼ cup (60 ml) mirin
¼ cup (60 ml) soy sauce
4 tbsp. sesame paste
¼ tsp. grated garlic
Drop Chinese hot chili oil

Combine dashi, mirin and soy sauce in a saucepan over low heat. Bring to a gentle simmer. Immediately remove from heat and cool to room temperature.

In a medium bowl, combine the sesame paste, garlic and hot chili oil and blend well with a whisk. Pour the dashi mixture into the bowl little by little, whisking continuously until the consistency is fluid but still somewhat thick. Serve as a dressing alongside a colorful arrangement of various ken-cut vegetables.

Cabbage chiffonade

Cabbage can also be cut into thin, needle-like strips. As in the ken-cut technique, cutting across the fibers makes softer strips, while cutting along the fibers results in crisper ones. Cabbage needle strips are popular as a side dish to meat entrees in Japan, and is especially seen alongside *tonkatsu* breaded pork.

1, 2. Discard any coarse or damaged outer leaves from a head of cabbage. Remove about ten outer leaves and cut out the thick white section at the base of each leaf.

3, 4. Stack the leaves together and roll them up tightly from the top down.

5, 6. Slice the roll as thinly as possible, relying mainly on the weight of the sharp usuba to pass through the leaves as the knife moves toward the far side of the board. Use immediately or cover tightly and refrigerate, as the shreds will dry out quickly.

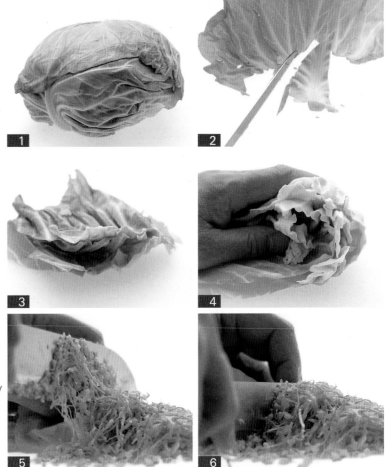

Cabbage and Beef *Shabu-shabu* Salad

SERVES FOUR

12 oz. (320 g) thinly sliced beef (for shabu-shabu)

1 medium head cabbage

Dressing

1 cup (240 ml) *dashi* stock (p. 34)

2 tbsp. and 1 tsp. rice vinegar

2 tbsp. and 1 tsp. soy sauce

1 tbsp. (3 g) *katsuobushi* bonito flakes

Combine all dressing ingredients in a small pan and bring to a simmer. Remove from heat and pass through a fine-mesh sieve. Cool to room temperature and set aside.

Take off cabbage leaves one at a time until about half the cabbage is left. Cut away the thick core at the base of each leaf, and stack the leaves up with the grain in the same direction. Chiffonade as described above, cutting the leaves against the grain to make soft shreds. Crisp in ice water and drain well.

Fill a medium pot with water and bring to 150–160°F (65–70°C) over medium heat. Add the beef slices in a small batch. Stir gently with cooking chopsticks to prevent the beef slices from sticking together. When the surface of the slices turns from red to a slightly whitish pink (as shown in picture), immediately plunge them in ice water to stop cooking and drain.

Roll the beef slices tightly and serve with the cabbage and dressing.

Sasagaki whittling

This shaving technique is used on long, fibrous vegetables such as *gobo* burdock root, carrots, or even asparagus. The technique is slightly similar to sharpening a pencil or whittling a stick. More than one length can be shaved at a time if the pieces are placed side-by-side on the cutting board and rolled back and forth together with the free hand while shaving the tips.

Burdock root, shown in these photos, is often cut *sasagaki*-style for *kimpira*, a classic vegetable side dish. Carrots and other long, thin vegetables can be cut sasagaki-style as well; asparagus is used to make a kimpira variation in the recipe at the end of the section.

Cutting burdock root
sasagaki-style

1. Use a brush to scrub the burdock root under cold running water. Rinse off any dirt. There is no need to peel the root. Cut off both ends; if it is long, cut it in half.

2. Make several shallow cuts down the length of the root, so that shavings will come off easily.

3, 4. Position the burdock horizontally, holding it with the free hand. Turn the cutting edge of the knife away, and use the tip to begin shaving the root while rotating it with the left hand, a little like sharpening a pencil. The cutting motion should be very short and quick.

For thinner shavings, a very sharp knife is needed. The angle of the blade should be nearly horizontal, and the cutting edge should just graze the burdock root. Handle the knife lightly. For thicker shavings, use a little more pressure and a slightly steeper blade angle.

5. Place the shavings in a bowl of cold water before cooking to remove harshness and to keep them from discoloring.

Cutting asparagus
sasagaki-style

6. After trimming the asparagus, make several straight cuts down the length of each asparagus spear, just as you would for burdock.

7, 8, 9, 10. As asparagus is not perfectly round, it won't roll smoothly like a burdock root or a carrot. Hold the stalk in your free hand and turn it back and forth while whittling the stalk down to the tip.

Sautéed Asparagus, Celery and Bell Peppers

SERVES TWO TO FOUR

4 stalks green asparagus, shaved *sasagaki*-style

½ stalk celery, thinly sliced on the diagonal

1 red bell pepper, seeded and sliced into thin strips

1 yellow bell pepper, seeded and sliced into thin strips

2 tsp. roasted sesame oil

Pinch chili flakes

1 tbsp. sugar

1 tbsp. soy sauce

Heat the roasted sesame oil in a saucepan over high heat. Add the asparagus, celery and bell peppers and cook for a minute. Stir in the chili flakes, sugar and soy sauce. The vegetables should release a fair amount of moisture. Continue to cook until the liquid is reduced and the vegetables are tender, but still a little crunchy.

Chasen-giri Tea-whisk Cut

The bamboo whisk used to whip powdered green tea and hot water into froth during the tea ceremony is called a *chasen*. Since eggplant cut in this style resembles a tea whisk, the cut became known as *chasen-giri*. Used almost exclusively on *nasu* Japanese eggplant, chasen-giri serves two purposes. Not only does it give the eggplant an attractive appearance, but it also serves to help the eggplant soak up the stock in which it is simmered.

Here the skin of the eggplant is scored at approximately ¼ inch (6 mm) intervals. The skin may also be scored at closer intervals, which creates a beautiful effect when cooked.

1. Remove the leaves of the eggplant by scoring them shallowly at the base and pulling them off. The stem should be left intact.

2, 3, 4. Insert the heel of the blade at the bottom of the eggplant and slide the knife slowly along the natural curve of the fruit. It helps to hold the base of the blade firmly between your thumb and index finger. Take care to maintain an even depth when scoring from the bottom to the top of the eggplant, and be sure not to cut all the way to the center of the fruit. Repeat this cut at regular intervals around the eggplant.

Simmered Eggplant and Chicken Breast

SERVES FOUR

4 *nasu* (Japanese eggplant), cut *chasen-giri*-style

8 oz. (240 g) chicken breast, skin-on

1 in. (3 cm) knob of ginger, peeled

½ bunch fresh spinach

2 cups (480 ml) *dashi* stock (recipe p. 34)

2 ⅔ tbsp. soy sauce

2 ⅔ tbsp. sake

2 tbsp. sugar

Vegetable oil for deep-frying

Cut the chicken breast into bite-size pieces. Peel the ginger and needle-cut across the grain (see p.33). Blanch the spinach in salted boiling water and shock in ice water. Lightly squeeze out the water from the spinach and set aside.

Heat the oil to 340°F (170°C). Deep-fry the eggplant until cooked, about 3 minutes. Shock in ice water, drain and lightly squeeze out excess water. Set aside.

Blanch the chicken pieces in boiling water for 15 seconds and shock in ice water. Drain, blot dry and set aside.

Combine the dashi stock, soy sauce, sake and sugar in a medium saucepan and bring to a simmer. Adjust the heat to medium, add the chicken pieces and cook for 5 minutes. Add the eggplant. Cook, turning the chicken and eggplant occasionally, until they absorb the dashi mixture well. Place the spinach in a bundle at the side of the pan and leave for about a minute to absorb the dashi mixture. Remove, lightly squeeze out the liquid, and cut into 1-inch (3 cm) lengths.

Place the eggplant on a serving plate, pinching the tops gently to enhance their tea-whisk shape. Arrange the chicken pieces, spinach and ginger strips, and spoon the dashi mixture over.

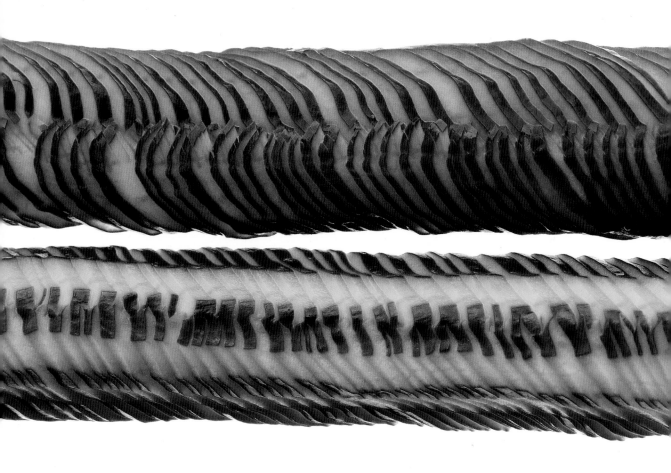

Jabara-giri Serpent's Belly Cut

The *jabara* (serpent's belly) cut is used almost exclusively for Japan's long, slender *kyuri* cucumbers. This cutting method makes the cucumber malleable like an accordion, and tenderizes the flesh without affecting the cucumber's crispness and succulence. Some people like to partially skin the cucumber (as seen in the lower photo above) to add visual and textural interest. Besides being attractive, cucumbers cut in this way hold flavorful dressings and marinades well. The recipe at the end of the section uses a vinegar-based marinade to make a classic *sunomono*. Jabara-cut cucumber also makes a lovely garnish to complement grilled dishes.

In executing this technique, it's important never to cut more than halfway into the cucumber. A good way to control the blade is to hold it at an angle with the tip downward. The tip of the knife—but never the heel—stays in contact with the cutting board as the blade moves down the length of the cucumber.

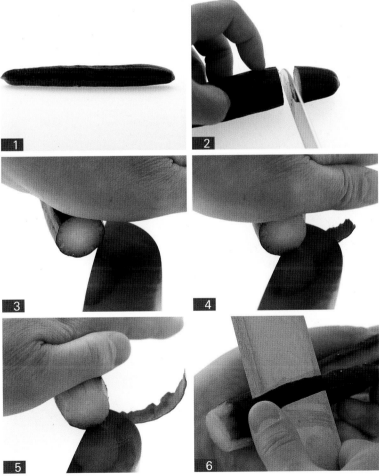

Cutting a cucumber
jabara-giri-style

1. The skin at the end of the cucumber where the stalk was attached usually has a bitter taste. It's best to remove both the stem end of the cucumber and the skin that surrounds it.

2, 3, 4. Cut off the stem end of the cucumber. Position the cucumber so the cut end is under the free hand at the base of the thumb. Place the knife tip under the cucumber with the blade towards you and cut into the skin. Flatten the angle of the knife slightly. With the free hand, gently roll the cucumber backward. Without changing position, move the knife along with it, keeping steady pressure against the cucumber to cut away the skin. Remove the skin all the way around the cucumber, making a slightly beveled edge.

5, 6. To improve texture and appearance, some cooks like to peel strips of skin down the length of the cucumber, creating alternating green and white stripes.

7, 8, 9. Place the cucumber on the cutting board. Try to find a place where it won't roll. Begin making diagonal cuts at narrow, regular intervals, being careful not to cut more than halfway through the cucumber.

A good way to control the depth of the cut is to raise the heel of the knife slightly and keep the tip in contact with the cutting board as you cut. To make the cuts more regular, curl the index finger of the free hand and press the fingertip joint against the side of the blade. Use this pressure to guide the knife and control the spacing of the cuts.

Carefully turn the cucumber end over end and place with the uncut side facing up. Repeat the process, making opposing diagonal cuts halfway through the cucumber on the reverse side.

10. Now the cucumber is pliable, like an accordion.

11. Soak the jabara-cut cucumber in salted water (1 cup / 240ml water and scant 1 tsp. salt) with a piece of *kombu* kelp for at least 30 minutes. This pulls moisture out of the cucumber, which helps keep the marinade or dressing from becoming watery.

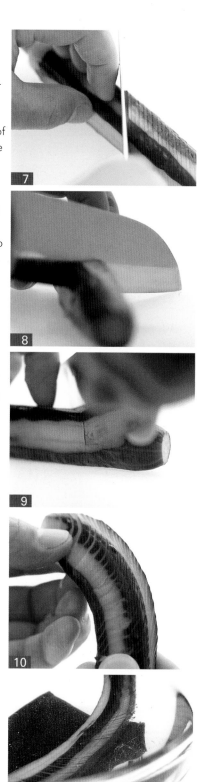

Vinegared Cucumber with Chicken Tenderloin

SERVES TWO TO FOUR

1 Japanese cucumber, cut *jabara-giri*-style

Salt and water

1 piece dried *kombu* kelp, 2 in. (5 cm) square

1 chicken tenderloin

2 tbsp. rice vinegar

3 tbsp. *dashi* stock (p. 34)

1 tbsp. mirin

1 tbsp. light soy sauce

1 radish

Four 2-inch (6 cm) squares *katsuramuki*-cut *daikon* radish, ⅛ inch (3 mm) thick

Place the cut cucumber and kombu in a bowl of salted water (1 cup / 240 ml water and scant 1 tsp. of salt) and leave for 30 minutes. Remove the cucumber and allow it to dry on a cloth or paper towel.

Meanwhile, place the chicken tenderloin in a saucepan and add cold water to cover. Heat until tiny bubbles begin to appear in the pan, indicating that the water temperature is between 175 and 190°F (80 and 90°C), and cook for 25 minutes. Allow to cool, then shred by hand.

Combine the rice vinegar, dashi stock, mirin and soy sauce in a non-reactive saucepan and bring to a gentle simmer. Set aside to cool to room temperature. Marinate the cucumber and chicken in the vinegar mixture for 20 minutes.

Cut the radish into a long ribbon, katsuramuki-style, and then cut into ken needles (see p. 32). Crisp the shredded radish in ice water, remove and blot dry.

Cut the cucumber crosswise into four pieces. Arrange cucumber, chicken and radishes on top of the daikon squares in individual dishes, and spoon the vinegar mixture over.

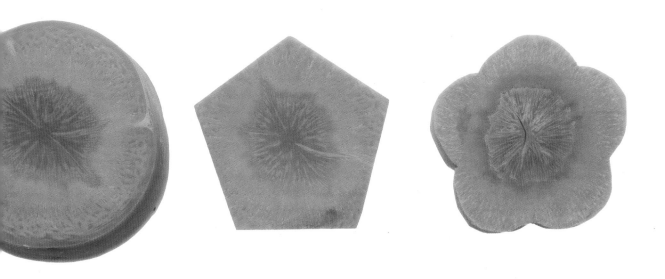

Kazari-giri
Decorative Vegetable Carving

Since Japanese chefs consider the appearance of food to be as important as its flavor, it's not surprising that *kazari-giri*, decorative cutting, has an essential place in the culinary tradition. On a basic level, cutting always creates decorative shapes—from perfect thin squares and hexagonal slices to the beveled edges on cylinder-cut vegetables. Kazari-giri, however, also refers to more fanciful techniques for cutting vegetables in the shape of various flowers and other items such as fans. *Ume-giri*, one of the simplest of these cuts, is demonstrated here. Short lengths of carrot and daikon are cut into slices shaped like *ume* plum blossoms, which are a symbol of early spring. Any firm vegetable, such as potato, radish, or jicama, can be carved in this way.

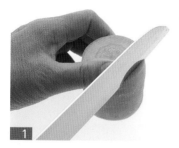

Cutting a carrot
ume-giri style

1. Cut a 3-inch (8 cm) length from a carrot. Use the *katsuramuki* technique (p. 26) to remove a thick outer layer of skin, making a cylinder. You are going to cut the cylinder into a pentagon shape.

Stand the carrot on end and hold it steady with your free hand as you make a shallow ¼-inch (6 mm) deep cut along the right side.

2. Now turn the blade of the *usuba* so that it is perpendicular to the side of the carrot. Make a shallow cut into the side to meet the first cut at right angles.

3. Repeat this five times, creating a five-sided shape. This cutout will serve as a guide for cutting down the sides of the carrot to make it pentagon-shaped.

4. Turn the carrot on its side. Using one side of the pentagon as a guide, cut all the way down the length of the carrot.

5. Repeat on the four remaining sides.

6. This five-sided length of carrot is the base for carving the blossom.

7, 8. Begin to carve the petals of the blossom. Start by making a ⅛-inch (4 mm) deep incision all the way down the length of the carrot at the center of each flat side.

9, 10. From the high point (corner of the pentagon) make a curved cut downward and away from you to reach the bottom of the incision. Repeat four times, rounding off the leading edges of five petals.

11, 12. Turn the carrot end-over-end and round the petals from the other side.

Continue to turn the carrot end-over-end, cleaning up the surface to define the shape of the petals better.

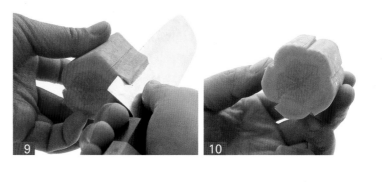

13, 14. Lengths of *daikon* radish can also be sculpted in this manner.

To use the blossoms in a soup (such as *suimono* or *o-wan* in kaiseki cuisine), cut the vegetables into ¼-inch (6 mm) thick slices. For the vegetable canapés on the next page, make very thin slices, about ¹⁄₁₆-inch (1 to 2 mm) thick.

15. Fold a damp towel and lay a blossom slice on it. Indent the center of the blossom by pressing on it with the rounded end of a wooden tool. Repeat for each blossom.

16. Place the blossoms in a bowl of ice water. They will float to the top.

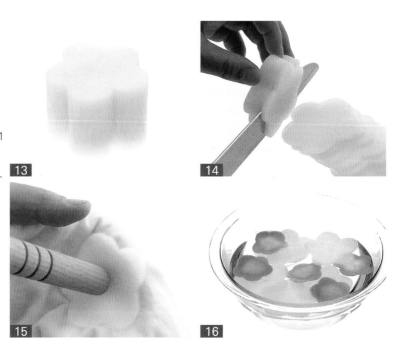

Vegetable Canapés

A variety of ingredients can be used to make these attractive canapés. Those shown on the left plate, from top to bottom, include the following:

1. Salmon Roe and Asparagus
Blanch delicate baby asparagus tips in salted boiling water for 60 to 90 seconds, then place them on the vegetable slices with a dollop of salmon roe.

2. *Unagi Kabayaki* Barbecued Eel and Cucumber
Peel and grate a small Japanese cucumber. Squeeze out excess water and add salt to taste. Cut the kabayaki into small squares. Arrange the cucumber and kabayaki on top of the vegetable slices.

3. *Mentaiko* Spicy Cod Roe
Top the vegetable slices with a dab of mentaiko spicy cod roe.

4. Cucumber and Grated *Daikon* Radish
Cut a small Japanese cucumber into thin slices. Core the center as needed. Blanch briefly (30 seconds) in salted boiling water. Grate the daikon radish and squeeze out the excess liquid. Mix with beaten egg yolk. (Basic ratio is 1 cup drained daikon and 1 beaten egg yolk.) Season with salt to taste.

5. *Ankimo* Monkfish Liver
Generously sprinkle the monkfish liver with salt and let stand for 15 minutes to remove any blood. Mix 1 quart water with 3 tablespoons salt (quantities can be adjusted to match the size of the liver). Place the liver in the salt water for 1 hour. Grind the liver to paste and put a dollop on each vegetable slice, topping with a small square of *nori* seaweed if desired.

*The top canapé shown on the dish on the right is monkfish liver and a square of nori.

THE DEBA

The deba knife was originally developed and forged in Sakai, the port town near Osaka. Some of the earliest knives made there were designed for cutting tobacco, and they were so well suited to the task that the Edo feudal government officially recognized their quality. Thereafter, knives made in the area received the appellation *Sakai kiwami*, and became a sought-after brand.

The deba is mainly used for cleaning and filleting fish and dressing poultry and other meats. The most notable feature of this knife is the heaviness added by the wide spine. This lends the stability and extra heft needed to cut through tough joints and thick bones with ease. The heel of the blade is used for chopping and cutting through bones. When extra force is needed, the fist of the free hand may be used to push down on the spine near the handle.

Certain of the deba's features make it ideal for filleting. For example, the width and steep angle of the *kiriba* blade path allow the knife to slice smoothly through the flesh without sticking, even though the blade is very broad. The shape of the *kissaki* tip, which curves toward the apex of the blade, is also important. The thick spine of the deba gradually becomes thinner toward the tip, allowing a great deal of freedom in manipulating the blade. The pointed kissaki also adds sensitivity during filleting; for example, it is possible to feel the kissaki touching the bones, and hear the tic-tic-tic sound made as the knife is drawn across them. Ideally, the entire blade should be used when filleting, but the area from the center to the tip is particularly important for this task.

Josei deba, 8.4 inches (210 mm). Awase, *aogami* steel with black water buffalo-horn collar and *honoki* wood handle. (Aritsugu)

The heavy blade requires a handle with some heft to match, so the wooden handle is relatively large, creating a good balance. It is important to keep a firm and stable grip when doing heavy work with the deba, so take a few moments to find the correct balance when handling the blade. The center of gravity should be on the bottom edge of the blade, not toward the kissaki tip.

This knife comes in several different varieties. The standard deba, or *hon-deba,* is an all-around heavy-duty dressing and filleting knife. A popular variation, the *mioroshi* deba, (literally, "filleting deba"), has a thinner blade and a narrower tip than a standard deba. It is not meant to cut through tough bones, but is for cutting a fillet into pieces.

The *ai-deba* is thinner and lighter than a hon-deba, but more substantial than a mioroshi deba. The ai-deba is not suitable for cutting through the hard bones of large fish, but can be used for dressing medium-sized fish with softer bones such as *saba* mackerel. It is also well suited for filleting. "*Ai*" means "both"; the ai-deba functions both as a cutting and filleting knife.

The *ko-deba* or small deba is often used to fillet smaller fish such as *aji* horse mackerel, and it is sometimes called called *aji-deba,* or *aji-kiri.* The aji-deba is especially common in areas near the sea, where aji is prepared by butterflying and partially drying the flesh. The aji-deba is also useful for filleting small freshwater fish such as rainbow trout.

Regardless of the particular type, awase-forged deba are generally preferable to honyaki-forged blades. Because of the heavy demands made on the deba in chopping and cutting through tough materials, the flexibility and resistance to chipping offered by an awase-forged knife is most desirable. For professionals, a standard deba about 9-½ inches (24 cm) long is best. For home cooks, about 8 inches (21 cm) is an ideal length.

LEFT: The same knife as that on p. 52.

CENTER: *Josei* ai-deba, 7.0 inches (180 mm). Awase, *shirogami* steel with black water buffalo-horn collar and *honoki* wood handle (Aritsugu)

RIGHT: Ko-deba, 4.2 inches (105 mm). Awase, SK-4 steel, black water buffalo-horn collar and honoki wood handle (Seki Magoroku Kinju/Kai)

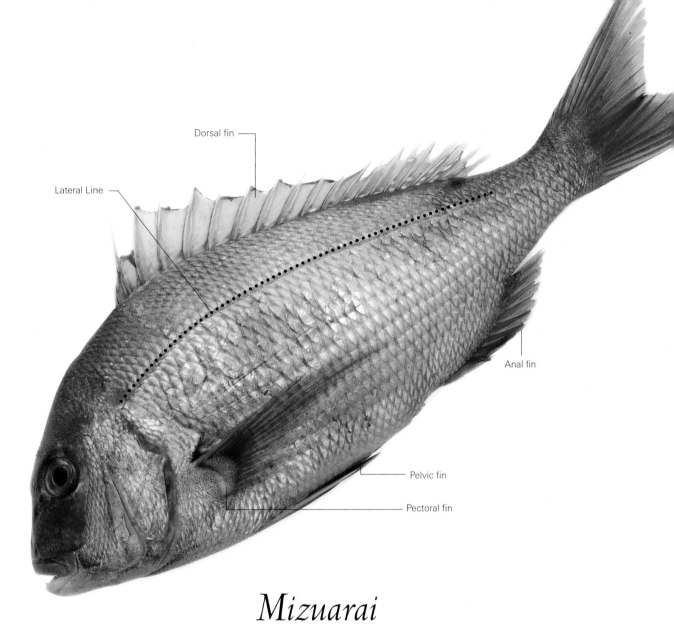

Dorsal fin

Lateral Line

Anal fin

Pelvic fin

Pectoral fin

Mizuarai

In filleting any fish, the first step is the cleaning procedure or *mizurarai*, which literally means "washing with water." Mizuarai includes scaling the fish, removing the gills, removing the internal organs, and, if desired, cutting off the head. It is of course a given that the knife should always be sharp, but gutting is particularly cumbersome with a dull blade.

It is ideal to use a three percent saltwater solution (the same salinity as sea water) to wash the fish after gutting, as this maintains the texture and flavor of the flesh. However, tap water is also acceptable. Prepare the salt water before beginning the mizuarai process by mixing a gallon (4 L) of cold water with ⅔ cup (120 g) salt. Have a separate basin ready for washing the fish. The fish will be washed twice, so don't use all the saltwater the first time.

It is helpful to understand the anatomy of a fish (page 55, photo 11 on page 57, and page 150) before gutting. For example, both ends of the gills are firmly attached to the body, and must be cut at each attachment. It is important not to puncture or cut the internal organs when cleaning the fish, as bitter fluids may seep out and ruin the flavor of the fish. In addition, the internal organs, especially the liver, are a delicacy; they are prepared in a variety of ways depending on the type of fish. Cured or marinated organs are called *chinmi*, which means "rarefied flavor." Japanese cooks hate to waste even a little bit of meat, so they use the entire fish, from head to tail, cutting it carefully and accurately into separate components and preparing each part accordingly.

It is best to carry out the *mizuarai* cleaning procedure next to a sink so the knife and cutting board can be kept clean during this process. Most professionals keep a couple of damp kitchen cloths close by to wipe down the knife and board after each step is completed. A brass *uroko* scaler is useful for hard-scaled fish like sea bream, though the serrated edge of a bottle cap may be used in a pinch. Since hard-scaled fish are messy to scale, it's a good idea to do it inside a large plastic trash bag.

Scaling

1. Position the fish with the head facing to the left, belly side toward you. Handle the fish with care. Like many round fish, *tai* sea bream have sharp, hard spines in the dorsal fin that can cause a nasty wound. Always move your hand in the direction of the tail when touching the fins. The scales are also hard and stubbornly attached, so an *uroko-hiki* brass scaler is the best tool for the job.

1. Holding the head firmly, insert the pectoral fin into the gill cover as shown, or cut it off.

2. Move the scaler from tail to head. It is best to work in a line along the body of the fish, starting along the lateral line. Move downward to scale the belly, then scale the upper side.

3. Don't neglect areas that are easy to miss, such as around the mouth and fins.

4, 5. To ensure that scaling is complete, run the tip or heel of the *deba* over the fish to catch any stray scales. Wash the fish in a basin of salt water or under cold running water to rinse off any debris. Blot thoroughly to dry.

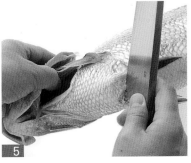

Cutting the gills at the throat

6, 7, 8. Position the fish on the board with its head to the right and the belly facing you. With the tip of the knife, make an incision under the gills to the center of the body, then turn the knife blade parallel to the body and cut the belly side from throat to anal orifice. The knife should pass between the pelvic fins. Take care not to cut too deeply so that the inner organs are not punctured.

9, 10, 11. Next, remove the gills. The gills are attached at one point at the throat and another at the base of the skull. The gills are also connected to the esophagus. (Photo 11 shows a detailed view of the gills). To free the gills, cut them where their "ends" are attached and let them stay with the esophagus. First, cut the attachment at the throat end.

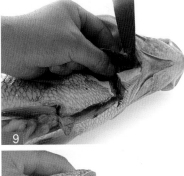

Cutting the gills at the base of the skull

12, 13. Pull the gills aside slightly to make way for the knife. Insert the knife deep into the head and cut the gills at the upper attachment (A). (Photo 13 clearly shows the base of the skull where the gills were attached.)

14. Holding the fish open with the left hand, take hold of the gills and innards with the right hand and gently pull them out from top to bottom.

15. Run the tip of the knife along the spine on the inside of the cavity to pierce the swim bladder and blood pockets of the kidney.

16. Pour salt or tap water into a broad tray or basin. Place the fish in the salt water and use a toothbrush to clean the cavity, brushing away the bloody debris. When all the bits have been removed, discard the water and rinse the fish well in the remaining salt water.

17. Thoroughly blot both the inner cavity and the outside of the fish dry with a towel.

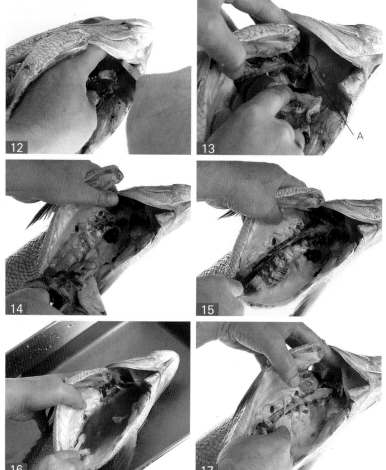

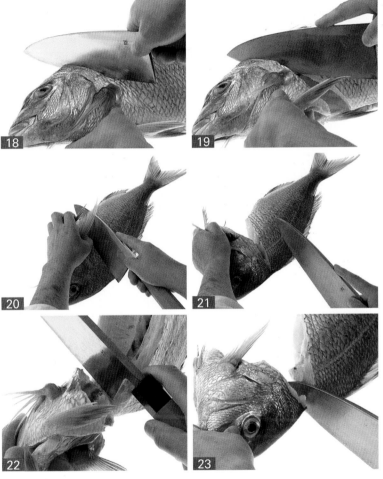

Removing the head

The head can be removed or left on, depending on how the fish is to be prepared. For example, in Japan, fish is grilled and served head-on for special occasions. Most of the time, however, the head is removed; while the body is cut for simmering or grilling, or thinly sliced into sashimi, the head is cut apart and used to make stock or simmered on its own. (See p. 60)

18, 19. Position the fish so the head is to the left, belly facing you. Insert the knife on a diagonal near the base of the pectoral fin. Angle the blade slightly toward the head. Cut down to the belly, penetrating the fish about halfway.

20, 21. Turn the fish so the spine faces you. Insert the knife on a matching diagonal and slice down to meet the first cut.

22. Use the heel of the knife to sever the thick bone of the spine near the crown of the head.

23, 24. Cut off the head completely. This concludes the *mizuarai* process.

Dividing the Head

Fish heads, generally discarded as trash in the West, are prized by Japanese chefs. For one thing, they make a wonderful stock for soups and sauces. When prepared as a dish on their own, fish heads are generally braised or simmered. The tender cheeks are considered a delicacy, as is the soft jelly around the eyes. Since fish heads contain many bones, they are divided into pieces, making them easier to consume. To eat, suck away the tender flesh and spit out the bones.

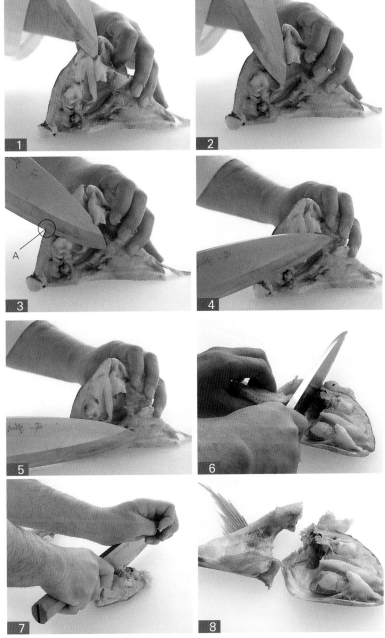

Cutting the head in half

In order to clearly show the position of the knife, this technique is shown with the fish head already cut in half. As noted below, exercise caution when holding the head with the left hand to avoid getting cut. One good trick for getting a secure grip on the head is grasp it with a clean terry-cloth towel.

1, 2. Holding the head with the left hand, insert the tip of the knife in the mouth. Press to push it in more deeply.

3, 4, 5. Push the tip further into the head, then begin cutting downward, using more of the blade. As you cut through the head, the tip of the knife will not move much; it acts a fulcrum as the blade moves downward. The force should be applied in the direction of point A in the photo. Use caution as the blade comes down; it is awfully easy to slice the thumb of the left hand. When the knife is almost parallel to the board (photo 4), cut through to the base.

6, 7, 8. Divide the halved head into the desired number of pieces, usually about five (see photo 10). If desired, the fins can be removed first, though it's fine to leave them on.

9, 10. Each half of the head is divided into five pieces, as shown in photo 10. The head has hard bones and joints that are difficult to penetrate. Use the heel of the knife to get through them. Holding the knife firmly, add extra force by pushing on the spine of the blade with fist of the free hand.

11. These pieces are great for making broth. The simmered flesh is also delicious. Before cooking, fish head pieces are usually sprinkled with salt to remove excess moisture and fishy odors.

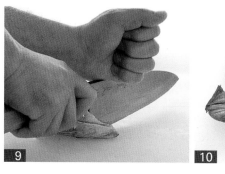

Braised *Tai* Sea Bream Head with Turnips

SERVES TWO TO THREE

1 tai head, cut into 10 pieces
Salt (for sprinkling tai head)
1 qt. (1 L) water (for blanching tai head)
Salted boiling water (for blanching turnips)
2 to 3 *kabu* Japanese white turnips
2 ½ cups (600 ml) water
3 tbsp. light soy sauce
3 tbsp. mirin
1 piece dried *kombu* kelp, 2 in. (5 cm) square
Yuzu peel, cut into slivers

Lightly sprinkle the tai pieces with the salt and let stand for 20 minutes. Meanwhile, bring the 1 qt. (1 L) of water to a boil in a saucepan. Place the tai pieces in the boiling water for 30 seconds, then shock in ice water. Remove any scales. Blot dry and set aside. Peel and cut the turnips into halves and blanch in salted boiling water.

Place the tai pieces, blanched turnips, water, soy sauce, mirin, and kombu in a suitable saucepan and bring to a simmer over medium heat. Simmer with a drop-lid (*otoshi-buta*) until the turnips are tender, about 15 minutes. Arrange in a serving bowl with the simmering liquid. Top with slivered yuzu peel.

To eat, pick out the tender flesh with chopsticks or put a piece of fish in your mouth and suck away the meat, spitting out the bones. It's fine to use your hands—this is why the Japanese have damp *o-shibori* towels at meals.

Sanmai Oroshi Three-piece Filleting
PART 1

Sanmai oroshi (cutting into three pieces) yields two fillets and the skeleton. This is a basic, yet versatile, technique for filleting fish. Though it may take some practice, using a single blade to fillet the fish results in beautifully clean fillets with minimal wasted flesh. In the West, the knives used for filleting are flexible, and bend around the bones. In filleting with a *deba* knife, which is thick and heavy, it is vital to control the angle of the blade and to slice the flesh away from the bones in wide sweeping strokes, using the entire blade. Don't use a sawing motion or limit slicing to the tip of the knife. The spine of a fish is lozenge-shaped, not flat, and the ribs are curved. The flesh is cut away most efficiently by angling the entire knife along these surfaces in smooth, sweeping cuts.

Cutting the first fillet from the belly side

1, 2. Position the fish diagonally so the head end is on the upper right, with the belly facing you. Place the free hand on the fish to keep it steady and insert the knife in the belly at the head. Hold the knife with the index finger on the spine to guide and stabilize the blade. Cut along the belly just above the pelvic and anal fins to the tail. Try to use the entire blade and slice as close to the rib bones as possible so as not waste that flesh. Repeat this sweeping slice. It helps to use the free hand to lift the flesh as you cut.

3, 4. Make three or four repeated long, sweeping cuts until the knife reaches the spine.

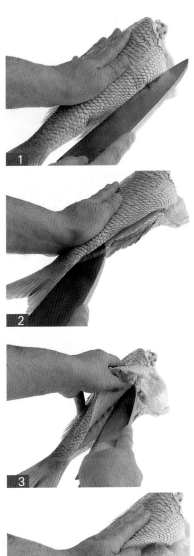

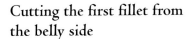

65

Cutting the first fillet from the back side

5. Turn the fish 180 degrees, so the dorsal fin is facing you and the tail is on the right.

6, 7. Using the entire knife blade, draw the knife in a long cut from the tail to the head end, slicing just above the dorsal fin. As before, use the free hand to hold the fish steady. You can use the left hand to gently push the fish toward the knife, tilting it slightly upward, which makes cutting easier.

8, 9. Repeat this long slicing cut, using the left thumb to raise the cut flesh away from the knife, until the knife reaches the spine from the other side. Typically, this drawing cut should be repeated two or three times.

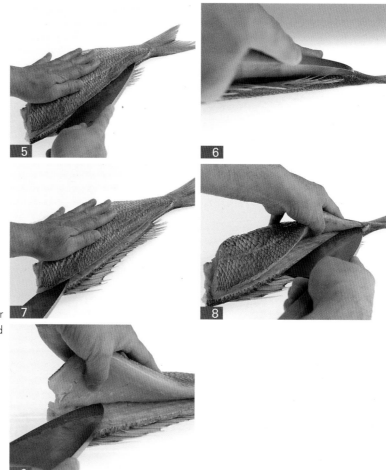

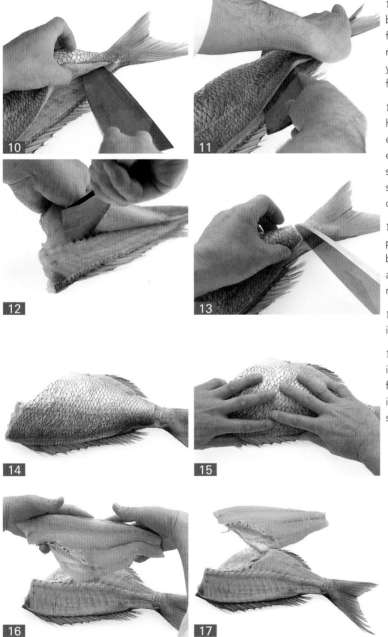

10. Insert the tip of the knife with the blade facing the tail to make a space for the knife along the spine, but do not cut the fillet away from the tail yet. Remove the knife and turn it to face the other way.

11. Hold the tail end with the left hand. Re-insert the knife at the tail end with the blade facing the head end, and slide the knife along the spine to cut the fillet away from the spine. (Gently pulling the tail in the opposite direction makes this easier)

12. When the knife reaches the tough part of the spine it will not be possible to continue. Gently open the fillet and use the tip of the knife to cut the remaining flesh from the spine.

13, 14. Cut the fillet at the tail end so it is now completely off the bone.

15, 16, 17. The fillet may be fragile, so it's wise to handle it carefully. Cup the fish fillet with both hands as shown in picture and turn it over, placing it skin-side down.

Cutting the second fillet from the back side

18. For the second fillet, start from the back side. Place the fish diagonally with the dorsal fin facing you and the tail on the lower left.

19, 20. Make a shallow cut along the upper side from head to tail, slicing just above the dorsal fin.

21, 22. Make repeated long sweeping cuts, using the whole of the blade and lifting the flesh away from the knife with the left hand as before, until the knife reaches the spine of the fish.

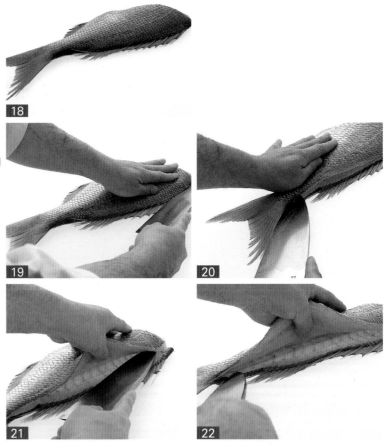

23

24

25

26

27

28

29

Cutting the second fillet from the belly side

After cutting the flesh away from the bones on the belly side, the second fillet can, like the first, be removed by sliding the knife along the spine (as in photos 10 to 13). However, some chefs prefer the alternative method detailed in step 27 below, which makes it easier to keep the fillet intact.

23. After completing step 22, position the fish diagonally with the tail at the upper right and the belly facing you. Make a vertical cut at the tail.

24, 25, 26. Cut along the belly from tail end to just above the anal fin. Try to slide the knife just above the bones to maximize yield. Make a series of long sweeping cuts, as before, until the knife reaches the spine.

27. Still working from the belly side of the fish, slide the tip of the blade along the spine. In a series of three or four passes, work the knife over the bone of the spine and beyond until the fillet is free. Carefully slide the knife along the spine from the tail to the head end to cut away the flesh.

28. When the blade reaches the tough part of the spine near the head end, raise the handle of the knife a bit and use the tip to cut around the irregularly shaped area of the spine. Cut the flesh away from the rib bones.

29. Cup the second fillet with both hands and gently turn it over, placing it skin-side down. You now have *san-mai*: two fillets and the skeleton.

Removing the belly bones and storing the fillets

30. Using the tip of the knife with the blade facing up, cut the ends of the belly bones from the flesh. Steady the knife by making a V shape with the index finger and thumb of the left hand and placing the spine of the knife in that V. This helps push the knife up and along the belly bones.

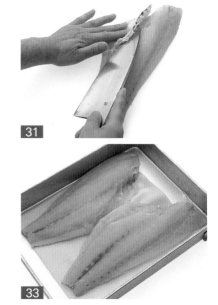

31, 32. Now hold the knife normally, with the index finger of the right hand on the spine of the knife to keep it stable, and thinly slice off the belly bones. The pin bones can either be removed now or just before the fillets are to be used.

33. The fillets should not touch any metal surfaces when they are stored. Place them in a paper-lined container, skin-side down. The fillets may be covered or wrapped with paper. This also keeps them from soaking up the liquids that seep out as they sit. To prevent drying, cover the container with plastic wrap and refrigerate before using.

Grilled *Tai* Sea Bream with Scallions

SERVES TWO

Two 4-oz. (120 g) *tai* fillets, skin-on

½ cup (120 ml) soy sauce

½ cup (120 ml) mirin

½ cup (120 ml) sake

½ bunch scallions, sliced paper-thin

*Other fish recommendations:

Porgy, snapper, sea bass, branzino, yellowtail, cod, salmon, tilefish and pompano

Remove the pin bones from the fillets and lay skin-side down in a wide, flat-bottomed container. Mix the soy sauce, mirin and sake and pour over the fillets to cover about halfway. Refrigerate for 30 minutes, turning once. Remove from marinade and lightly pat dry.

Skewer the fillets and place on the grill skin side down. Allow to grill undisturbed until the edges of the skin side are well-browned. Turn and grill the other side for three or four minutes. Blanket the top with scallion slices. If possible, place the fillets under a salamander or broiler and cook for one minute. Serve immediately.

Sanmai Oroshi Three-piece Filleting
PART 2

For practicing your *sanmai oroshi* technique, It is best to start with fish that have soft scales and bones, such as *saba* mackerel (shown here) or *sawara* Spanish mackerel. There is no need to worry about scaling with an *urokohiki* brass scale-remover or removing gills and hard fins. Also, mackerel, with their long, slender bodies, produce thick fillets that can be cut fairly quickly. Some chefs feel that it is important not to damage the tender flesh of soft fish like mackerel, and are careful not to turn them during filleting. This is the technique shown here. Others follow the same sanmai oroshi process as for *tai* sea bream, turning the fish over after the first fillet is removed.

The following steps include a simplified *mizuarai* process for scaling and gutting the fish. This mizuarai can be done in the sink, as soft-scaled fish are less messy to scale and gut than hard-scaled fish like *tai* sea bream.

Mizuarai

Before beginning, prepare a 3% salt water solution by mixing a gallon (4 L) water with ⅔ cup (120 g) salt.

1. Position the fish with its head to the left. Holding the head with the left hand and the *deba* with the right, use small strokes of the blade to gently scrape the scales away, moving from the tail to the head. Take care not to pierce the flesh. When the scales have been removed from the first side, turn the fish over and scale the other side. Rinse the fish in a basin of salt water or under cold running water and dry well with a paper or cloth towel.

2, 3. With the head to the left, place the knife on a slight angle, positioned to make a diagonal cut behind the pectoral fin (photo 2). Insert the blade and pull the knife towards your body to cut halfway through the fish. Flip the fish so it is now upside down, with the head still on the left. Insert the knife behind the pectoral fin on a diagonal matching the previous cut, and draw the blade toward you. This will remove the head.

4. Lay the fish with the tail end to the left.

5, 6, 7. Extend the right index finger along the spine of the blade for stability as you hold the knife, and place the left palm gently on the fish to keep it from slipping. Use the middle part of the blade to make a shallow cut along the belly to the vent opening. Remove the innards.

8. Gently holding the fish open with the left hand, scrape along the spine with the knife tip to remove the dark red blood line of the kidney. Wash in salt water and thoroughly blot the surface and cavity with a paper towel.

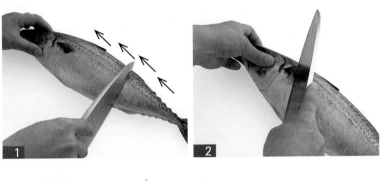

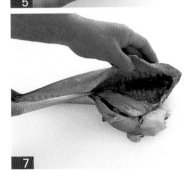

Cutting the first fillet from the belly side

9. Position the fish so the tail is to the left and the belly is facing you.

10, 11. Placing the left palm gently on the fish, with the right index finger extended along the spine of the knife to stabilize the blade, make a long slice along the belly all the way to the tail. Try to use the entire blade, not just the tip, as this makes for a better cut. Repeat this sweeping cut two or three times until the blade reaches the spine.

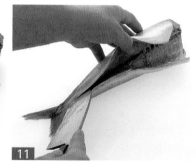

Cutting the first fillet from the back side

12. Turn the fish 180 degrees so that the tail is on the right and the back is facing you. Slice along the centerline from the tail to the head end in two or three strokes, until the blade reaches the spine. It helps to use the free hand to raise the flesh away from the knife slightly as you work.

13. Make a space for the knife by inserting it between the spine and the upper fillet at the tail, with the blade facing the tail. Remove the knife without cutting the fillet from the tail (see p. 67). Turn the knife so that the blade faces the head end, reinsert it at the tail, and slide it along the spine towards the head to release the fillet from the spine. Cut the tail end to remove the fillet.

14. Handle fillets by gently cupping them with both hands (see p. 67).

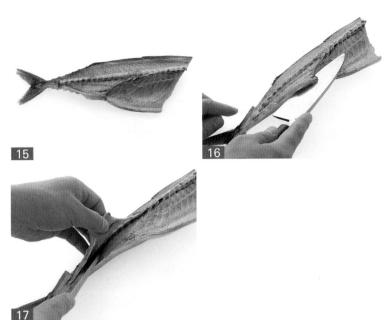

Cutting the second fillet from the belly side

15. Position the fish so that the tail is to the left, with the skin side down.

16, 17. Extending the index finger along the spine of the knife for stability, use a drawing motion to slice between the rib bones and flesh from head to tail. This cut should start from the middle part of the knife blade and end at the tip of the knife.

Cutting the second fillet from the back side

18, 19. Switch the fish so the tail is on your right. Using the entire blade from heel to tip, slice the flesh away from the rib bones. Work from the tail to the head end, holding the ribcage open, to make this deep cut.

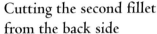

Removing the second fillet

20, 21. Insert the knife blade between the rib bones and flesh, facing the tail. Remove and reinsert so the blade is facing the head end. Slide the knife along the spine from tail to head end to cut away the bones. Finally, insert the knife facing the tail and cut the end of the fillet to completely separate the bones from the fillet.

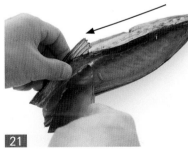

22. Now you have *sanmai* (three pieces): two fillets and the skeleton.
  The belly bones, which are usually removed just before preparing sashimi, are left intact for vinegared mackerel in the recipe that follows. To remove the belly bones from mackerel for grilling, etc., please refer to p. 70.

Vinegared Mackerel

SERVES TWO TO FOUR

2 mackerel fillets
½ cup (100 g) granulated sugar
¼ cup (50 g) salt
About 2 cups (480 ml) rice vinegar

* *Saba* mackerel or *sawara* Spanish mackerel may be most commonly available, but *aji* horse mackerel works well too. Curing and marinating times should be adjusted depending on the size and fat content of the fish (i.e., longer for larger or fattier fish).

Place the fillets skin-side down on a flat mesh sieve, such as the *takezaru* bamboo sieve shown here, and dust liberally with sugar. Sugar absorbs the excess liquid from the fish, removing strong odors without imparting flavor (salt, which has smaller molecules, also removes

liquid, but penetrates the flesh of the fish and makes it salty). Let the fillets stand at room temperature until the excess liquid is absorbed (usually about 40 minutes for a 12-inch / 30 cm mackerel fillet). Rinse in cold water and blot dry thoroughly.

Place on a flat mesh sieve and sprinkle generously with salt (this step absorbs additional liquid while adding saltiness). Let stand for one hour. Rinse in cold water and blot dry.

Place the fillets in a non-reactive container, pour the rice vinegar to cover a little over halfway, and cover with a kitchen towel to keep the vinegar from evaporating. Leave until the surface of the fillets turns slightly white, usually about 20 minutes.

Remove from the vinegar and gently pat dry with paper towels. Do not rinse. To prepare as sashimi, see p. 116.

Daimyo Oroshi Straight Filleting

Daimyo oroshi is a faster technique than *sanmai oroshi*. Rather than taking the four steps required for sanmai oroshi—cutting from the belly and from the back on each side—daimyo oroshi removes the flesh in a single cut from head to tail on each side. Of course, this method leaves more flesh on the bone. *Daimyo*, the feudal lords of old Japan, were considered extravagant, so this cut, which is more wasteful than sanmai oroshi, is named after them.

Daimyo oroshi is used in preparing small or slender fish such as *iwashi* sardines (shown here), *aji* horse mackerel, small mackerel, *sanma* Pacific saury, or *kisu* Japanese whiting.

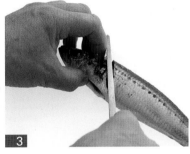

1, 2. The same simplified *mizuarai* process outlined for mackerel on p. 73 can be used to clean smaller fish. Use the tip of the *deba* to gently scrape off the scales, moving from the tail to the head. Rinse under cold running water to remove any stray scales.

3. Take off the head with a single diagonal cut running just behind the pectoral fin.

4, 5. For small fish like sardines, there is no need to leave the belly intact; it is mostly skin with little meat underneath. To remove the innards, cut on the diagonal to take a wedge from the underside of the fish (photo 4). Remove any remaining bits with the tip of the knife or the little finger.

Use a fingernail to remove the blood line that runs along the underside of the spine. Rinse the fish in salt water and blot dry inside and out.

6. Position the fish so that the head end is on the right, belly facing you.

7, 8, 9. Insert the center of the blade at the head end. In a single smooth motion, draw the knife along the spine to the tail. Hold the fish gently with the left hand to steady it without pressing too hard. After reaching the tail, finish the cut by slicing through the skin at the end. Remove the fillet.

Turn the fish over, keeping the head on the right side, and repeat to cut the second fillet.

10. You now have *sanmai*, or three pieces—two fillets and a carcass—cut with the *daimyo oroshi* technique. This technique is known as straight filleting in English.

11. To remove the belly bones, see p. 70. For small fish like sardines, there is no need to remove the pin bones as they are soft enough to eat.

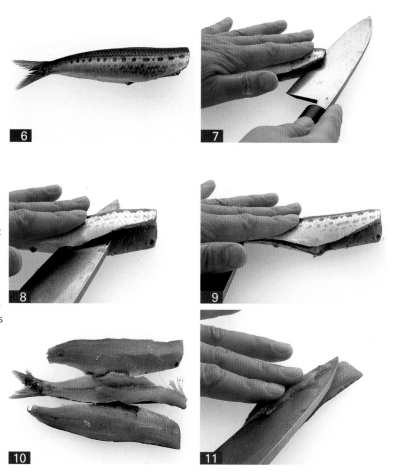

Grilled Cheddar Sardines

SERVES TWO

Two 8 in. / 20 cm *iwashi* sardines, cut into fillets, skin-on

Salt (for sprinkling sardines)

2 slices cheddar or other sharp cheese

1 egg yolk, lightly beaten

Other fish recommendations: squid, *kisu* Japanese whiting, *sayori* Japanese halfbeak

Lightly sprinkle the fillets with sea salt and leave for 10 minutes. Rinse in cold water and blot dry. Preheat a grill or grill pan. Place the fillets skin-side down and grill for 3 to 5 minutes, or until the fillets are cooked halfway through. Turn the fillets and grill for 2 to 3 minutes, until the fillets are almost cooked. Preheat the broiler. Transfer the fillets skin-side down onto an oven sheet lined with aluminum foil. Place a slice of cheddar cheese on top of each fillet and broil until the cheese melts slightly. Remove the fillets from the broiler—still on the oven sheet—and baste with beaten egg yolk. Return to the broiler until the egg-yolk glaze is dry. Repeat the basting and broiling process twice more. (This allows the protein in the egg yolk to coagulate and makes a bright yellow glaze on the fillets and cheese.) Serve immediately.

Hiraki Butterflying

There are innumerable ways of preparing fish in Japan. One of the most popular is to make *himono*—semi-dried fish, cured with salt, that are broiled or grilled over hot coals. *Hiraki*, or butterflying, is the way himono are prepared before curing. This method keeps the fish in a single piece while opening the maximum possible surface area for drying.

Tsubonuki is a method for removing the gills and innards through the gill cover with a pair of disposable chopsticks. This technique is used for small or medium fish such as *nijimasu* rainbow trout (shown here), *hokke* Atka mackerel, *mebaru* rockfish and *ayu* sweetfish. It is particularly useful when the head is to be kept on during cooking.

It is important to note that the tsubonuki gutting technique can only be used on very fresh fish. If the fish is too old, the internal organs soften and break very easily, and cannot be pulled out with chopsticks.

Gutting via the gill cover (*Tsubonuki*)

1. Scale the fish from tail to head as in the shortened *mizuarai* process on p. 73.

2. Lay the fish on its back with the head facing to the right. Take it in the left hand, belly-side-up, and open the gill cover with your fingers. Use a pair of disposable chopsticks to pinch the gills, which look like a red "collar" under the gill cover. Hold the gills between the chopsticks and push them into the body cavity of the fish.

3, 4. Twist the chopsticks a few times so that the innards and gills are wrapped around them, then pull the entire mass out. Place the fish in salt water and scrape out any remaining bits with the chopsticks.

5. Rinse the fish well in a fresh bath of salt water and pat dry.

Butterflying

6. Position the fish diagonally with the tail to the upper right, the dorsal spine facing you, and the head to the lower left.

7, 8. Make a single cut along the centerline of the fish just to the upper side of the dorsal fin. Use the entire length of the blade to slice open the fish along the back from tail to head. Be extremely careful not to cut too far and slice into the belly of the fish.

9. Reposition the fish so it is belly-down, with the head facing you. Raise the handle of the knife so it is nearly vertical and place the tip against the back of the head. Use just enough downward pressure to cut through the top of the head, stopping when the blade reaches the tongue.

10. The fish can now be opened completely so that it lies flat.

11, 12. The spine and rib bones are removed by cutting the area shown inside the rectangle in photo 10. First turn the fish skin-side up, with the tail to the left. Slide the knife along the back of the fish just above the dorsal fin, moving from head to tail. Repeat this long cut several times, raising the flesh to expose the bones further, until the bones are just separated from the flesh.

13. Reverse the blade so it faces the head, and cut off the strip of bones at the head end.

14. The fish is now butterflied and ready to cure.

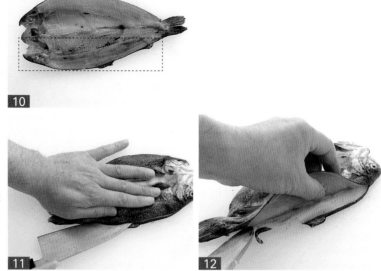

Grilled Semi-Dried Rainbow Trout

SERVES TWO

2 rainbow trout (about 8 in. / 20 cm long),
   butterflied, skin-on

Salt

4 tbsp. mirin

2 tbsp. soy sauce

10 *shiso* leaves, slivered

In a wide flat-bottomed container, add 2 tsp. salt to 2 cups (480 ml) water to make a 2% saltwater solution. Refrigerate the butterflied fillets in this solution for an hour. Remove and pat dry. Lay the fillets skin-side down on a rack and air-dry overnight (at least 8 hours).

Combine mirin, soy sauce and slivered shiso. Grill the fillets skin-side down (if broiling, start skin-side up) on high heat for 3 minutes, brushing with the shiso mixture from time to time. Turn them over and grill 4 minutes more, brushing on the shiso glaze periodically. Serve immediately.

Don't be afraid to try to eat *himono* with chopsticks. Simply grasp the flesh, pin bones and all, between the tips of the chopsticks and eat. If you find a few bones on your tongue, it's fine to discreetly spit them out as you are eating. In fact, smaller bones can often be eaten as they are—the high heat used for grilling himono dries them completely, making them not only edible, but crunchy and delicious. The crisp browned skin is also a treat.

Gomai Oroshi Five-piece Filleting

The *gomai oroshi* technique produces four fillets (the fifth "piece" refers to the skeleton or carcass that is left after the fillets are removed). This technique is used for flatfish such as flounder, fluke, turbot, halibut and larger fish such as bonito. Here, fluke was used to demonstrate the process. Flatfish have tiny scales, and some cooks don't bother to do more than scrub the fish well. However, it's best to take off the scales and a thin upper layer of the skin with a *yanagiba* knife.

Great care must be taken in the initial steps of cleaning the fish, especially when removing the head, so that the *nigadama*, or gall bladder, is removed intact. If the gall bladder is punctured, the bitter liquid inside will discolor the flesh of the fish and ruin its flavor.

The strips of meat closest to the fins, called the *engawa*, are considered a delicacy by sashimi fans because of their toothsome texture. Of course, sashimi made from the rest of the *hirame* fluke fillet is very popular as well. The entire fillet is suitable for deep-frying, as in the recipe for deep-fried hirame nuggets at the end of this section.

Mizuarai: Scale removing

Removing the scales by peeling with the knife is called *sukibiki*, which means "teasing." Bonito skin is also removed using this technique.

Prepare a 3% salt water solution by mixing a gallon (4 L) water with ⅔ cup (120 g) salt.

1. Position the fish so that the pigmented side faces up, with the tail to the left.

2, 3. The longer, thinner *yanagiba* knife is more suitable than the *deba* for paring away the tiny scales. Starting at the tail and moving toward the head with the blade away from you, pare away the scales together with a very thin layer of skin in strips as shown. Work outward from the centerline (spine) of the fish. Be careful not to cut all the way through the skin or nick the flesh.

4, 5, 6, 7. To remove the scales from the areas near the fins, it helps to grasp the fish by the tail, turning the body so that the area to be scaled lies flat under the knife (photo 4). You can also place your hand under the body of the fish to allow better access to these areas. Make full use of the length of yanagiba knife, using the tip or the heel as circumstances warrant.

8. When all the scales have been removed from the pigmented side, turn the fish over, keeping the tail on the left, and repeat the scaling process on the underside of the fish. Rinse the fish in a basin of salt water or under cold running water. Dry well with a paper or cloth towel.

87

Mizuarai: Removing the head and organs

9. Position the fish pigment-side up, with the head on the left. Remove the pectoral fin with a *deba* knife.

10. With the deba blade at a slight angle, make a diagonal cut from the top of the head toward the pectoral fin. Stop at about the line of the eye. Do not cut too far or you will pierce the gall bladder.

11. Turn the fish over, keeping the head on the left. Lift the pectoral fin and cut it off.

12. Cutting at what is now the bottom, again on a diagonal with the blade at a slight angle (see photo), match the previous cut.

13. Reverse the knife so that the blade is facing upward. Cut the skin in a shallow arc to the far side. Cutting with the blade upward ensures that the organs are not pierced. Use the left hand to lift the skin while cutting.

14. Pull the head gently away from the body to expose the organs. (The black globe in the photo is the gall bladder.) Put down the knife. Carefully hold the organs in the left hand while using both hands to turn the fish over, pigmented-side up.

15. Keeping the organs and the head together in the left hand, cut off the last of the skin connecting the head to the body.

16. Rinse the fish in salt water, using a toothbrush to gently brush away any leftover blood or tissue. Blot dry thoroughly with kitchen paper.

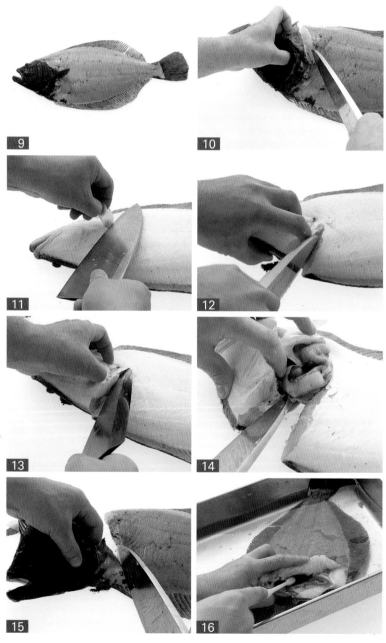

Cutting the edges of the fillets

17. For easier removal of the fillets, a shallow incision a must be made all around the fish along the fins. Start by making a shallow vertical cut at the tail.

18, 19. Using the V between the thumb and index finger as a brace, place the knife blade-up and begin to make a shallow cut around the circumference of the fish where fins meet flesh. Begin with the side of the fish that is closest. Working with the blade up may be a little awkward at first, but it ensures that the cut will not be too deep.

20, 21. When you begin making the incision around the part of the fish that is farthest away, use the groove between the index and middle fingers to steady and guide the knife. Work slowly and carefully, using the tip to make the cut. As you approach the head end of the fish, raise the handle to finish the cut (see photo 21).

Removing the fillets

22. Position the fish pigmented-side up, with the head away from you and the tail towards you. Extending the index finger along the back of the knife for stability, make a long, slicing cut along the centerline of the fish, where the spine is. Repeat this cut two or three times until the blade hits the bone.

23, 24. Starting at the head end, insert the tip of the knife at the left of the center cut, raising the flesh to expose the area to be cut. Cut away the flesh along the length of the spine first, then make progressively longer sweeping cuts to remove the fillet. Use the left hand to lift away the flesh for the next cut.

25, 26. In drawing these long cuts, use the entire knife blade while exerting minimal pressure beyond the weight of the knife. Slow and steady is best. Keep slicing until you reach your initial border cut around the circumference of the fish.

27. This makes the first of four fillets.

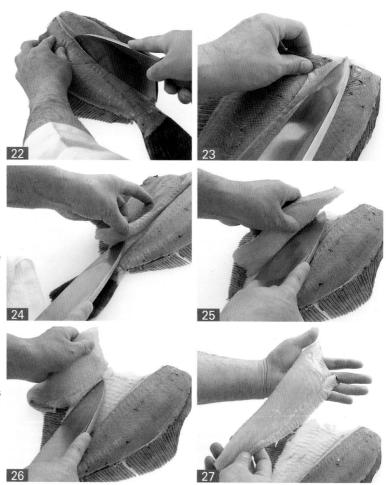

28, 29. Turn the fish so that the head is toward you and the tail is facing away, positioning it so it will be easy to cut the second fillet starting at the tail end. Insert the tip of the knife at the corner closest to the spine. As before, slice the flesh away from the bones along the spine toward the head end, using gradually larger sweeping cuts. Gently lifting the flesh to expose the next place to be cut, use the entire length of the knife and very little pressure.

30. Cut the fillet along the bones until initial circumference cut is reached. The fillet should lift away from the skeleton of the fish at that point. Keep going, little by little, until the entire fillet can be lifted off.

31. Turn the fish over so the white underbelly is facing up. The head end should be farthest from you, and the tail nearest you. As before, with the blade up, use the tip of the knife to make a shallow incision around the circumference of the fish where the fins meet the flesh. Repeat steps 17-30.

As there is more meat on the pigmented side of the fish, the fillets on the white underside will be thinner. This may make them a little more difficult to handle. It is important to use a light touch—you can "feel" the bones through the knife—and not rush the job. Listen for the rhythmic tapping sound the knife makes as it comes in contact with the bones.

32. *Gomai oroshi* is now complete. The fish is in five pieces: four fillets, and the skeleton they were cut from.

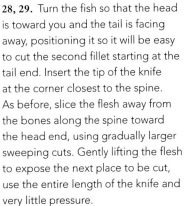

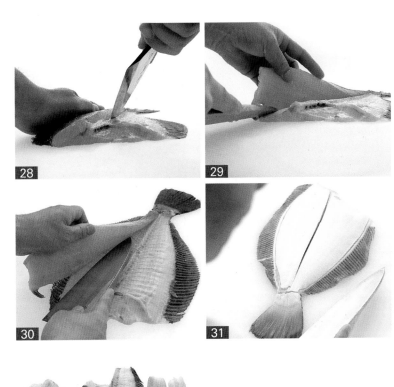

Removing the belly bones

33, 34. With the blade up, insert the tip of the knife under where the belly bones are attached to the flesh. Hold the fillet with your left hand and cut upwards to free the ends of the bones from the flesh.

35, 36. Reverse the knife and thinly slice underneath the bones. When you reach the end of the fillet, lift the bones away and cut the last bit of flesh to remove the bones completely.

37, 38. The *engawa* is the band of muscle that runs along the fins. Prized in Japan for its crunchy texture, engawa is often cut away from the rest of the fillet and served as sashimi. Separating the engawa from the flesh is simply a matter of finding the ridged strip of muscle, which is slightly more firm than the rest of the flesh, and cutting it away in a single long cut. The difference between the engawa and the rest of the flesh should be clear at a glance, but if in doubt cut about a finger's width away from the outer edge of the fillet.

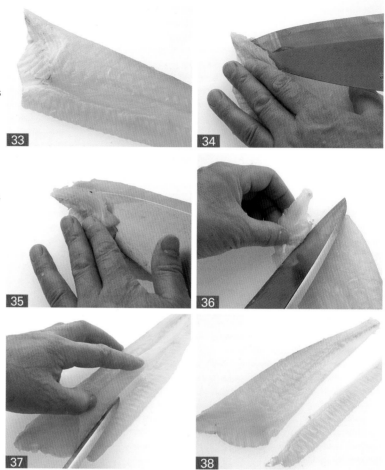

Deep-Fried *Hirame* Nuggets

SERVES TWO

2 medium hirame (fluke) fillets

4 tbsp. soy sauce

1 tsp. grated ginger

Potato starch or corn starch

Vegetable oil for deep-frying

4 asparagus spears, each washed, trimmed and cut into three pieces

Other fish r.ecommendations; turbot, plaice, summer flounder or other flatfish. Cod, mackerel, or sea bream can be used with equally delicious results.

Preheat the oil to 340°F (170°C).

Cut the fillets into 1 oz. (30 g) pieces. Combine the soy sauce and grated ginger in a small bowl. Place the fish pieces in the bowl and douse with the soy-ginger mixture. Dredge the nuggets in potato starch and deep-fry for about 4 minutes until crisp and golden-brown. Transfer to a paper-lined plate to drain any excess oil. Deep-fry the asparagus without flouring, for 30 seconds and drain. Serve immediately.

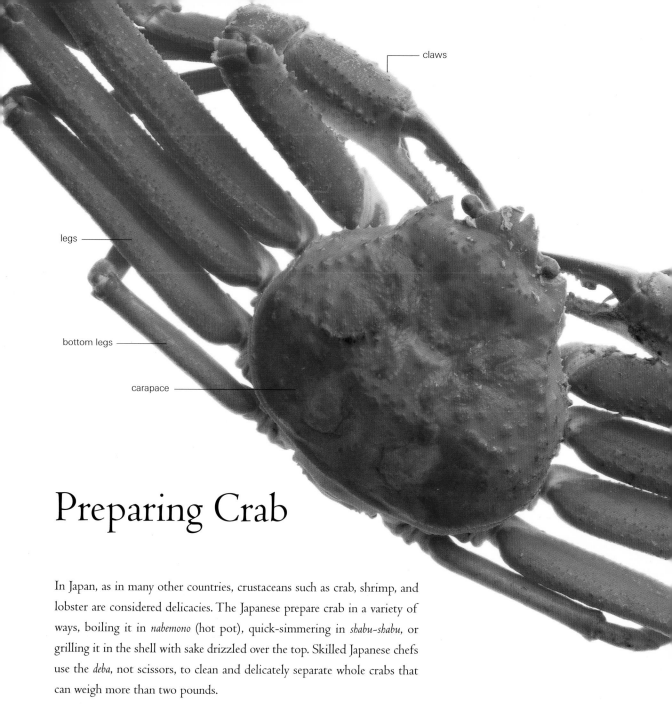

claws

legs

bottom legs

carapace

Preparing Crab

In Japan, as in many other countries, crustaceans such as crab, shrimp, and lobster are considered delicacies. The Japanese prepare crab in a variety of ways, boiling it in *nabemono* (hot pot), quick-simmering in *shabu-shabu*, or grilling it in the shell with sake drizzled over the top. Skilled Japanese chefs use the *deba*, not scissors, to clean and delicately separate whole crabs that can weigh more than two pounds.

This section features the *zuwai-gani*, or snow crab, which is in season during the winter months. The first step is to prepare plenty of boiling salted water (1 heaping teaspoon of salt per 2 quarts / 2 L water) to cook the crab. Lower the crab into the cooking water shell-side down, to prevent the innards from leaking out during cooking. If the body of the crab (without the legs) is around eight inches (20 cm) wide, boil for 10 to 15 minutes. If it is much smaller, five minutes will do. Cool the crab completely before beginning to take it apart.

shoulder

apron

Removing claws and legs

1. Using the heel of the *deba* knife, firmly tap the bottom joint of the claws at the point where the claw meets the shoulder. Remove both claws.

2. Use the tip of the knife to cut off both bottom legs. For the claws, little pressure is required.

3. Cut off the remaining three legs from the bottom joints in one stroke. Do the same on the opposite side.

4, 5. To remove the apron (abdomen), hold the crab body in the free hand and cut into the apron with the tip of the knife. This is a male crab, so the apron is relatively small compared to that of a female.

Separating the body from the shell

6, 7. Insert the tip of the knife between the carapace and the body. Press down on the carapace with the knife tip, creating enough space to remove the body with the free hand. Set shell aside.

8, 9. The white and gray spongy finger-like appendages at the front of the body are the gills. Though they are edible, they aren't tasty. Cut them off at the base and scrape them away with the tip of the knife.

10. Cut the body in half. This requires little force, since the shell here is thin and soft.

11, 12. To quarter each piece, press the edge of the blade against the center of the cut side. The index finger should rest lightly on the spine to help balance the blade.

13, 14. Keeping downward pressure on the piece, turn it so that it is standing on end, with the knife perpendicular to the cut side. Push the knife straight down, pressing the spine of the blade with the fist of the free hand to add force. Using a small fork or fine-tipped chopsticks, remove the meat, eggs and innards (as desired) from their papery casings.

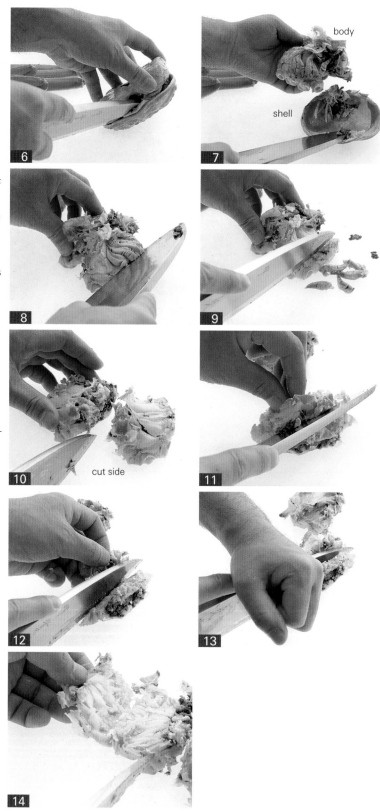

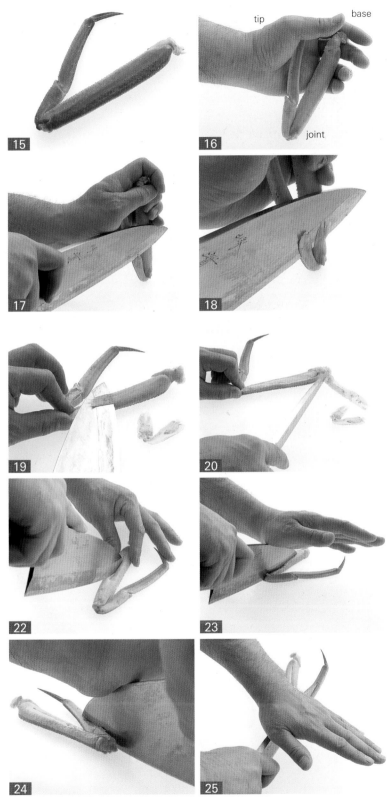

Preparing the legs

15, 16. Bend the leg and hold the tip and base together in the left hand.

17, 18. Rest the joint in a stable position on the cutting board. Use the tip of the knife to slice off the shell about 1 in. (2.5 cm) from the bottom, revealing the meat.

19, 20, 21. Lay the leg on the cutting board. Using the tip of the knife with the blade facing away, slice away a strip of shell. Rather than using a sawing motion, keep moving down the length of the knife blade while cutting through the shell. Pick out the meat and reserve the shell. Repeat with the other legs.

Alternate method for cutting legs

22. With the hard shell (pigment side) down, use the tip of the knife to score a line along the shell from top to joint.

23. The leg joint is hard. To cut through it, hold the knife firmly, wrapping the fingers of the knife hand around the handle, and press down on the spine of the blade with the free hand.

24, 25. Score the lower part of the leg from tip to joint, then press down on the hard joint again. The meat will be easy to remove from the slit in the shell. Repeat for all legs, reserving the shells.

Opening the claws

26 Position the claw pigment-side down, and use the heel of the knife to lightly press between the pincers, cracking them open.

27, 28. Hold the claw firmly and set the heel of the knife into it. Use the free hand to press on the knife spine, opening up the rest of the claw. The meat is easily removed from the crack. Pick out the meat, reserving the shells.

29. This method yields the carapace, the quartered body, and the meat and shells from the claws and legs.

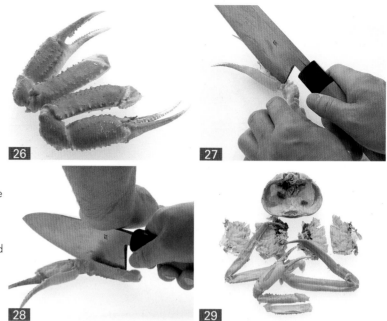

Crab and Arugula with Shell-flavored Vinegar Dressing

SERVES TWO TO THREE

1 boiled whole crab, about 2 lbs. (900 g)

3½ tbsp. water

1 tbsp. rice vinegar

1 tbsp. soy sauce (preferably light type)

½ tbsp. granulated sugar

1 bunch arugula, washed and trimmed

Cut the crab into pieces and remove the meat, eggs and innards from body and legs. Reserve the carapace and the shells from the legs. Discard the papery casings from the body of the crab. Combine the shells, water, vinegar, soy sauce and granulated sugar in a non-reactive saucepan. Bring to a simmer, then immediately remove from the heat. Let the liquid cool to room temperature, then strain.

If using the carapace shell as a serving dish, rinse and blot dry. Place the arugula, crabmeat, eggs and innards in the shell. Arrange the vinegar dressing in a small cup on the side.

THE YANAGIBA

The *yanagiba* is a long, slender knife used mainly to slice sashimi. Because of the length of the blade, very little pressure is needed when drawing it smoothly from heel to tip through the fish. Professional chefs use blades nearly 14 inches (36 cm) in length—nearly as long as a small sword—but they are skilled at using the entire length, and also have ample room to work. For the home chef, a blade about 12 inches (30 cm) long is more than adequate.

Japanese chefs have a huge range of cutting techniques at their disposal to enhance the flavor, texture and appearance of the food they are preparing. This is especially clear with sashimi, where the type of fish being sliced may determine which cutting technique should be used. (This is explained in further detail in the sashimi section on page 106.) In some cases, more than one cutting style is applied to a particular fish to highlight different

textures; *toro* fatty tuna belly, for example, may be cut into thick slices to emphasize its satisfying richness, and thin slices that bring out its exquisite melting texture. Served alongside each other, the different cuts contrast the outstanding qualities for which toro is prized.

The yanagiba is never pushed, but is rather drawn or pulled (in Japanese, the phrase for cutting sashimi is "*sashimi wo hiku*"—*hiku* being the verb "to pull"). In theory, the longer the knife, the less stress is put on the flesh.

Many variations on the yanagiba have been developed to cut specific kinds of seafood into sashimi. For example, the *fuguhiki* is used to slice *fugu* blowfish. It functions in much the same way as the yanagiba, but the blade and thickness of the spine are much thinner to facilitate slicing the elastic flesh of this fish into paper-thin slices.

Another sashimi knife called the *takohiki* is used mainly in the Kanto area

Yanagiba, 11.7 inches (300 mm). Honyaki, *shirogami* steel, mirror-finish. *Kokutan* ebony handle with a silver band. (Hiyoshimaru)

of eastern Japan. This square-tipped knife has a straight *shinogi* line and cutting edge. According to legend, in the Edo era, chefs who had to slice sashimi in front of nobles were reprimanded for pointing the sharp tip of the sword-like yanagiba at their betters, so the chefs began having knives made without a pointed tip. Regardless of the truth to this story, the straight cutting edge and squared-off tip of the takohiki are well-suited for cutting food into even squares. Still, this knife is rarely used outside of Kanto today; most chefs use a yanagiba to slice sashimi as the tip comes in handy for precision work.

The yanagiba is used for skinning as well as slicing. In Japanese cuisine, when fish are grilled, simmered, or sautéed the skin is generally left on and eaten. For sashimi, however, the skin is removed in most cases, which gives the fish a finer texture. In some fish, like sea bream, a beautiful red pattern is revealed on the flesh when the skin is removed. Fish in the yellowtail family are similar: in the winter, when they are at their peak, a paper-thin layer of white fat, like a dusting of snow, remains after the skin is removed. Natural gifts like these can be a beautiful accent in a sashimi arrangement.

From left: *Kengata* (sword-shaped) takohiki, 11.7 inches (300 mm). Honyaki, mirror-finish, *aogami* steel. *Kokutan* ebony handle with a silver band (Hiyoshimaru)
Takohiki, 11.7 inches (300 mm). Awase, aogami steel with black water buffalo-horn collar and *honoki* wood handle (Tsukiji Masamoto)

Skinning

The skin may be removed from fillets starting either from the left or the right end. If starting from the left, the blade should face to the right as the skin is pulled off, and vice versa. Regardless of direction, the skin should be removed from tail to head end.

The fillet is placed skin-side down, with the head cut end in the direction to be skinned. The first step is to cut a "grip"—a small piece of flesh to hold securely as the skin is pulled away. The knife should cut between skin and flesh in a sliding motion as the skin stretches in the opposite direction. Don't worry about cutting though the skin by mistake; simply start over from that point.

Preparing the fillet for skinning

1. For this demonstration we used fillets of *tai* sea bream (see p. 64 for filleting technique).

2. Place the fillets skin-side down. Cut each fillet in two by slicing down the spine line.

3. Trimming away the *chiai* red muscle fiber from the center area will give the sashimi a more delicate flavor.

Removing the skin from left to right

4. Position the fish with the tail end to the left.

5. Angling the blade slightly to the left, use the tip of the knife to make a small cut approximately ½ inch (1 cm) from the tail, stopping just above the skin. Do not cut all the way through the fillet. Use this knob of flesh as a grip, and hold the skin with the left hand. If the fish is slippery, use a cloth towel to secure your grip.

6. Pull the skin gently to the left while gradually turning the blade to the right. Be careful not to cut through the skin.

7. With the knife held nearly parallel to the board, slide it toward the head while making small up-and-down motions to cut between the skin and flesh. Keep the angle of the knife constant to avoid cutting off the skin or penetrating into the flesh. As the knife moves toward the head end, keep pulling the skin in the opposite direction.

8. When turned over, an expertly skinned tai fillet reveals a beautiful pattern.

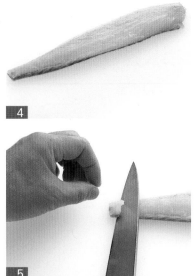

4

5

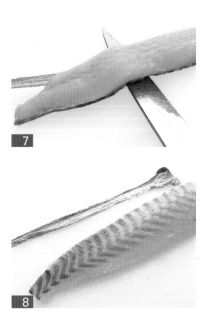

6

7

8

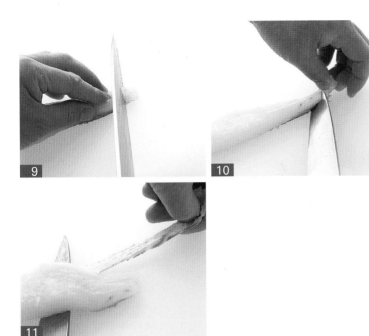

Removing the skin from right to left

9. Place the fillet skin-side down, with the tail end on the right. Angle the blade slightly to the right, then use the tip of the knife to make a small cut approximately ½ inch (1 cm) from the tail. Stop just above the skin. Do not cut all the way through the fillet.

10. Use this knob of flesh as a grip, and hold the skin with the left hand. Pull to the right to stretch the skin while gradually turning the blade to the left.

11. Remove the skin as detailed in step 7 above.

Removing the skin from the *engawa*

The engawa, removed from the fluke during filleting, can be skinned in the same way as the fillet. After skinning, cut pieces for sashimi as desired.

S A S H I M I

Sashimi is simply thinly sliced raw seafood served with different fresh vegetable garnishes and accents, ground wasabi, and a small dish of soy sauce for dipping. The delicate interplay of flavors and textures and the subtle differences in the taste of a given type of fish from season to season have elevated sashimi to an elite position among gourmets. Yet it is also hugely popular among the masses in Japan; cooks regularly buy fresh fish in the supermarket to slice and serve as sashimi at home. Indeed, there are few better ways to appreciate a really fresh fish than to eat it as sashimi.

A range of cutting techniques and variations may be used to bring out the best flavor, texture and appearance. The two most basic techniques are called *sogizukuri* (also called *sogigiri*) and *hirazukuri*. Sogizukuri is used to slice fish fairly thin, improving the texture; most types of fish are sliced sogizukuri-style for sushi. Fish with tougher flesh such as *fugu* blowfish are sliced extremely thin using a sogizukuri variation called *usuzukuri*. Since this technique requires the flesh to be cut into uniform paper-thin slices, it is not easy, but a sharp knife helps a great deal. Lastly, relatively fatty or soft-fleshed fish such as tuna and *tai* sea bream are often cut hirazukuri-style, in which

the flesh is cut into thick slices to deliver a substantial, satisfying mouthful.

There are also various ways to tenderize and improve the texture of chewy seafood like squid, or fish with a tough exterior like mackerel. Some of them have poetic names: *matsukasa-giri*, for example, means "pine-cone cut," since the scored surface of the flesh resembles a pine cone; *kanoko-giri*, spotted-fawn cut, recalls the markings of a baby deer. In the case of mackerel, even when the skin is removed, a silvery, slightly hard surface remains. *Yaezukuri*, or "doubled cut," is used to score this surface, making the fish easier to chew.

The arrangement of sashimi on the plate is based on the ancient Chinese concept of Yin-Yang, which expresses the interdependence of opposing forces in the natural world. The ground edge of the knife is considered yang; the opposite side is yin. Fish sliced *hirazukuri* style on the yang side are presented on a square or rectangular yin-style plate, while fish sliced with the *sogigiri* or *usuzukuri* technique on the yin side are placed on a circular yang-style plate. The slices are always arranged in odd-numbered groupings.

When presenting sashimi, the slices and garnish can be arranged to echo the natural scenery of a traditional mountain-river painting. Choose where you want the "front" of the plate to be, regardless of its shape, and make a mountain of *ken*-cut daikon radish on the far side. Then lay a *shiso* leaf, if you have one, against the side of the "mountain," and place the sashimi slices, overlapping and standing up as much as possible, to flow away from the mountain and around the plate. Edible garnishes such as wasabi leaves, *warabi* fern, purple shiso flowers, or shiso buds can be added to the arrangement as shown in the photographs. A mound of ground wasabi is always placed on the right-hand side of the plate so that it can be easily reached with chopsticks held in the right hand.

Sogizukuri Slicing

This fairly thin cut is good for slightly tough or fibrous fish, as it makes the flesh softer and easier to chew. The thickness of the *sogizukuri* (also called *sogigiri*) sashimi slices is adjusted depending on the kind of fish. With *sogizukuri* the angle of the knife can be adjusted to maximize the area of each piece, increasing yield.

This technique makes it clear why Japanese say *hiku*, "to pull," instead of "to cut" when slicing sashimi. The blade never pushes or cuts, but is rather drawn smoothly back without any added pressure.

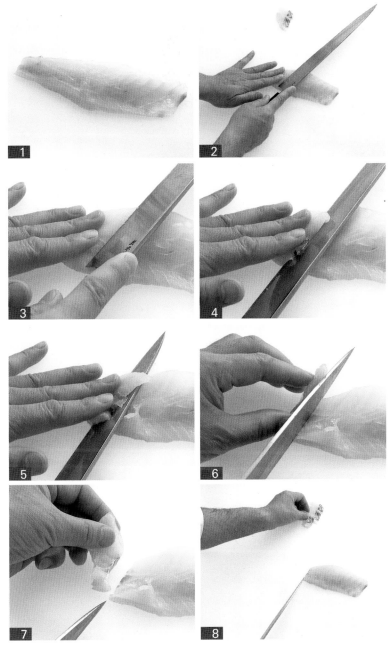

1. Position the fillet with the skinned side down and the narrower end to the left.

2. Place the heel of the knife on the fillet at about a 40-degree angle. The index finger should lie along the spine of the blade to control the strength and direction of the cut. The fingers of the left hand should rest very lightly against the fillet to steady it.

3, 4, 5. Draw the blade toward you while sandwiching the thin piece of flesh between the left hand and the blade. Pull nearly the entire length of the blade through the fillet to slice through.

6, 7. When the knife tip reaches the fillet, turn the blade to vertical and cut through the flesh completely. This creates a *koba* or ledge, which makes the cut look sharp and beautiful.

8. Gently pick up the piece and place it at the upper left of the cutting board. Repeat to cut through the entire fillet, placing the cut pieces together so that they can be counted easily.

Hirazukuri Slicing

This relatively thick cut is commonly used for softer, less fibrous fish.
Usually, the fillet is positioned with the head end on the right and the
tail to the left, so that the thinnest part of the fillet faces the front of the
board. It's best to place the fillet at the front edge of the cutting board.
The free space is needed to accommodate the length of the blade as it is
drawn through the fillet from heel to tip. If the fillet is in the center of the
board, the knife handle will get in the way. It's important to use the entire
length of the blade for this technique.

Hirazukuri

1. Lay the fillet at the front edge of the cutting board, skin-side up, tail end to the left.

2. Extend the index finger along the knife spine to control the pressure, direction and stability of the cut. Wrap the thumb and other fingers around the handle. Place the heel of the knife at a slight angle just in front of the edge of the fillet. The thickness of the cut is determined by the placement of the blade (here, the fillet is sliced into ¼ inch / 6 cm thick pieces).

3, 4. Drop the tip to about 45° to touch the fillet, then draw the knife toward you lightly, keeping the blade in constant contact with the fish and keeping the pressure consistent. As you pull the knife, imagine that you are describing a short arc with the tip. The blade should remain completely perpendicular to the board. The pivot point of the cut moves from the heel to the tip of the blade as it slices through the fillet; it is always at the point where the knife blade and the fillet meet. The drawing motion should be completed in a single rapid motion, cutting the fibers of the flesh cleanly. This will give the sashimi a glossy appearance.

5. When the cut is completed, draw the knife nearly to the tip and give it another brief tug to make sure that the piece is cut through completely.

6. Without taking the knife away from the cut piece, move the slice off to the right side of the cutting board, keeping the blade in contact with the board. If the slices are cut very thin, or the fish is flaky, leave the pieces undisturbed and continue cutting.

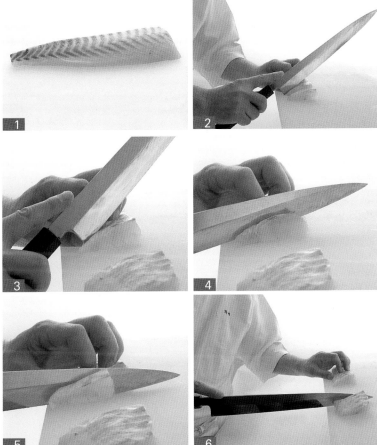

Usuzukuri Slicing

This technique is used for fish with firm, elastic flesh, such as *fugu* blowfish or freshwater fish, and for chilled fish. The technique is basically the same as *sogizukuri* (page 110), but the flesh is cut paper-thin. The blade should be visible through the flesh while slicing.

Matching food to tableware is an important element of Japanese cuisine. Since the thin slices of *usuzukuri* are transculent, a plate with a beautiful color or pattern lets guests enjoy the combined effect. It's also wise to prepare the sashimi immediately before serving, so the delicate slices don't dry out.

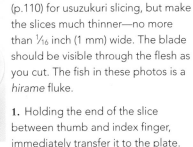

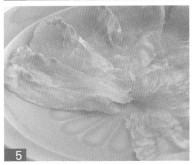

Use the basic *sogizukuri* technique (p.110) for uzuzukuri slicing, but make the slices much thinner—no more than 1/16 inch (1 mm) wide. The blade should be visible through the flesh as you cut. The fish in these photos is a *hirame* fluke.

1. Holding the end of the slice between thumb and index finger, immediately transfer it to the plate. Place one end near the rim of the plate and use the tip of the knife to lightly guide and position the other end toward the center of the plate. The plate shown, which is 8 inches (20 cm) in diameter (excluding rim) accommodated eleven usuzukuri slices. For larger amounts of fish, use a platter, arranging the slices like overlapping petals.

2. Slice off a second piece and place it next to the first one, overlapping the edges slightly.

3, 4. Keep moving the plate as you work, so that the space for the next piece is always easy to reach.

5. Leave room in the completed arrangement for a garnish. With *usuzukuri,* garnishes are often added as an accent to the plate. It's good to have an idea of where the garnish will go before beginning to arrange the sashimi.

Yaezukuri Doubled Cut

Yaezukuri is a *hirazukuri* technique used on fish that have a slightly tough skin or surface, such as *sawara* Spanish mackerel, *tai* sea bream, or *katsuo* bonito. (*Yae* refers to something doubled or multilayered; for example, *yae-zakura* are double-petaled cherry blossoms.) Yaezukuri is most commonly used on vinegared mackerel (page 76), as shown here. Because each piece of fish is scored across the top in both directions, the tough part is easier to chew.

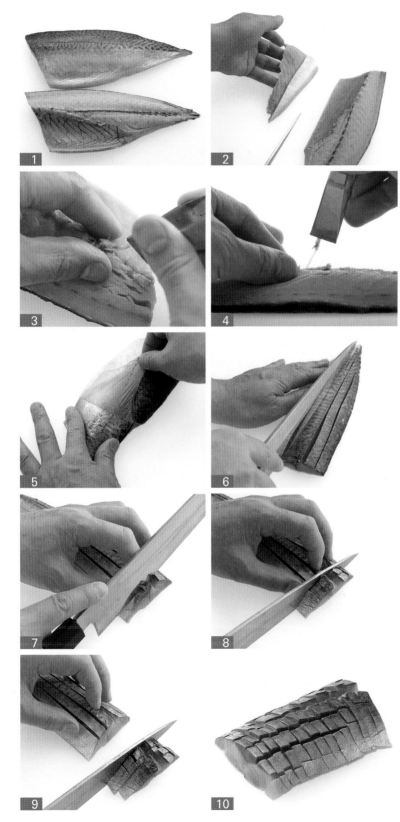

Removing pin bones and skin

1, 2. Prepare fillets of vinegared mackerel (see p. 76). Place one fillet skin-side down and slice out the belly bones as shown on p. 70.

3. Most fish fillets will have a few tough pin bones around the head end. They are embedded deeply into the flesh. Press the flesh slightly with the fingers to find the buried bones, and remove them with flat-tipped tweezers.

4. Remove the other pin bones. The bones lie in the flesh at an angle from tail to head. To remove, pull them out at the same angle (toward the tail) so as not to tear the flesh.

5. Turn the fish skin-side up. Grasp the thin skin at the head end and peel it back across the body from head to the tail. Pull it off evenly and slowly, keeping the hand close to the fillet so that the skin is less likely to tear.

Scoring

6. Keeping the skin side up, make four or five shallow parallel cuts down the length of the fillet. Cut only about ⅛ inch (3 mm) deep.

7. Turn the fillet so that the wide end is to the right. Using the *hirazukuri* technique (p. 112), make a shallow cut about ¼ inch (6 mm) from the head end.

8. Move the knife down ¼ inch (6 mm) and make a second cut, this time going all the way through the fillet. Slide the cut piece to the right with the knife.

9. Repeat steps 7 and 8, moving each piece to the right as it is cut.

10. The vinegared mackerel is now beautifully cut and ready to arrange for serving.

Matsukasa-giri Pine-cone Cut
Kanoko-giri Spotted-fawn Cut
Naruto-giri Spiral Cut

Matsukasa-giri means, literally, "pine-cone cut." The knife is inserted on the bias at an angle to make a lattice pattern. The seafood is then blanched and shocked in ice water, which makes the cuts open up to create the pine-cone effect.

Kanoko refers to the spots on the back of a fawn. For this effect, the cuts are made on the bias with the knife perpendicular to the board, to make a lattice pattern. Often used on squid, kanoko-giri is also used on ingredients such as abalone (an abalone steak sautéed in butter works very well with this cut), ark shell, and the base of bamboo shoots.

Naruto-giri literally means "spiral tide cut." Traditionally, squid is rolled together with *nori* seaweed and cut into spiral-patterned rounds. The photo shows naruto-giri with *shiso* leaves, which add a fresh, light flavor.

While these techniques make food more beautiful, they also enhance the texture of the ingredients, which is very important to the Japanese palate. There's even an expression, *hazawari* (literally, "food touching your teeth") that refers to the "bite" or consistency of food. Moreover, as these techniques also help retain sauces and dressings that might normally slide off slippery foods like squid, they work to enhance flavor as well.

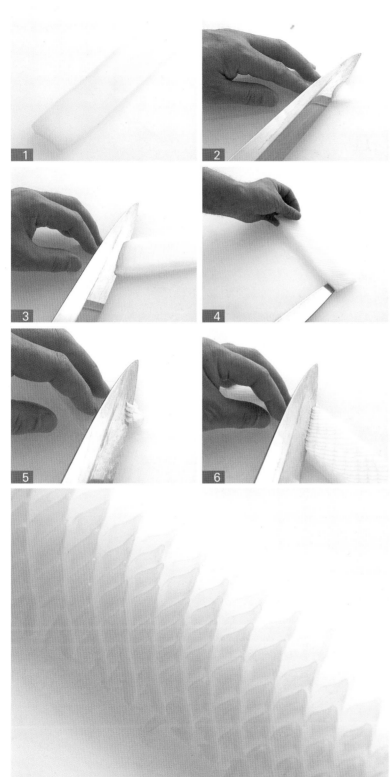

Matsukasa-giri

1. Place a rectangular strip of cleaned squid diagonally on the cutting board.

2, 3. With the blade facing away and at an angle nearly parallel to the board, draw the knife toward you to score the surface of the squid on the bias. Starting from the edge, score at intervals of about ⅛ inch (3 mm). Take care not to cut more than halfway through the flesh.

4. Carefully lift the squid, holding one end with the free hand, and place it on the opposite diagonal. (That is, lift the end on the lower left and place it on the upper left.)

5, 6. Score on the bias with the knife blade facing away and nearly flat to the board, starting from right to left. This should have the effect of cross-hatching your first set of score marks.

For sashimi, push the long edges together to make an arc shape and cut into bite-size pieces.

7. Pushing the long edges of the squid together causes the cut parts to bloom outward. For a more pronounced effect, blanch the squid in boiling water for a few seconds and shock in ice water before slicing. Cut into bite-size pieces.

Kanoko-giri

1. Place a rectangular strip of cleaned squid diagonally on the cutting board.

2. Holding the blade straight up and down (perpendicular to the surface), draw the knife toward you to score on the bias. Start at the right edge and move toward the left.

3, 4. Score rhythmically at approximately ⅛-inch (3 mm) intervals, taking care not to cut more than halfway into the flesh.

When you reach the end, carefully lift the squid, holding one end with your free hand and place it on the opposite diagonal (i.e., lift the end on the lower left and place it on the upper left).

Draw the knife toward you with the blade straight up and down to score on the bias at the same intervals as before. This should make a crosshatch over the first set of score marks.

5. Blanch in boiling water for a few seconds, then shock in ice water. Cut into bite-size pieces.

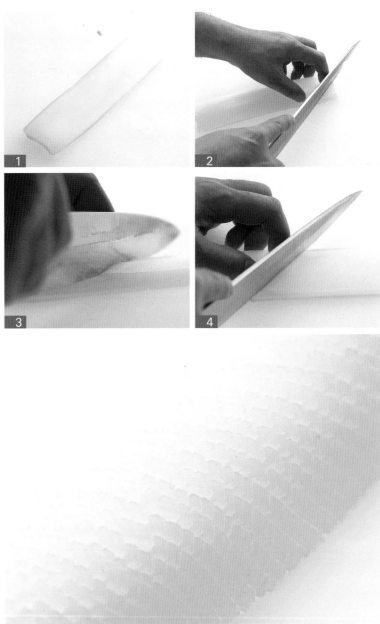

Naruto-giri

1, 2. Trim the cleaned squid into a rough square. Turn 90° so that the trimmed edge is at the top with the skinned side up so that the flesh will be cut along the grain.

3. Gently draw the knife across the surface from top to bottom to score the flesh at ⅛-inch (3 mm) intervals. Move from right to left, taking care not to cut more than halfway through the flesh. Try to make the depth of the cuts even by keeping the contact of the blade against the flesh consistent.

4. Turn the squid over. Arrange the *shiso* leaves on top, cutting them if necessary to fit the squid.

5. Roll the shiso and squid together, making sure that the score marks run lengthwise on the outside of the roll.

6. Position the roll seam-down and slice into rounds of any thickness desired.

A Knife for Every Function

The depth and variety of Japanese cuisine is reflected in the specialty knives its masters use. Each of these knives was developed for the sole purpose of preparing a specific Japanese specialty: sushi, grilled eel, *hamo* pike conger and *soba* buckwheat noodles, to name a few.

Shown here is the range of knives available from Kiya, a famous knife retailer in Japan. For definitions of the terms used in the descriptions, refer to the glossary on page 17 and the "Japanese Knife Materials" section on page 147.

1. *Mioroshi* Deba

Mioroshi means "filleting." This sleek deba, with its slender spine and profile, is optimal for filleting. The slightly narrow grip makes it easy to turn the knife while cutting.

■ From left: 10.5 inches (270 mm), 9.6 inches (240 mm) and 8.4 inches (210 mm).
Awase, Yasuki *shirogami* steel, black water buffalo-horn collar, *honoki* wood handle (Izutsuki brand)

2. Yanagiba (*shobu*)

This Kansai-style sashimi knife has a curved edge. *Yanagi* refers to a willow leaf, but this knife is also called *shobu*, or "iris leaf."

■ From left: 12.9 inches (330 mm), 11.7 inches (300 mm), 10.5 inches (270 mm), 9.6 inches (240 mm) and 8.4 inches (210 mm).
Awase, Yasuki shirogami steel, black water buffalo-horn collar, honoki wood handle (Izutsuki brand)

3. *Takohiki*

Like the yanagiba, this knife is for slicing sashimi. *Tako* means "octopus," and the takohiki is so called because its straight tip is very handy for cutting curled octopus legs. These days, however, the yanagiba is more popular.

■ At left: 12.9 inches (330 mm), honyaki, Yasuki shirogami steel, black water buffalo-horn collar, honoki wood handle (Izutsuki brand). Next three, from left: 10.5 inches (270 mm), 9.6 inches (240 mm) and 8.4 inches (210 mm).
Awase, Yasuki shirogami steel, black water buffalo-horn collar, honoki wood handle (Izutsuki brand)

4. *Hamokiri*

Hamo, a type of conger eel, has long, tough bones—too many, in fact, to remove. When the bones are finely chopped with this knife, which is especially long and heavy, hamo can be enjoyed in various ways, from sashimi to tempura, without removing the bones.

■ 11.7 inches (300 mm), awase, Yasuki shirogami steel, black water buffalo-horn collar, honoki wood handle (Izutsuki brand)

5. *Sushikiri*

The curved, double-ground edge of this knife is ideal for cutting rolled or pressed sushi. The tip is inserted first, and then pressure is put on the heel while cutting to utilize the curve of the blade.

■ 9.6 inches (240 mm), honyaki, Yasuki shirogami steel, black water buffalo-horn collar, honoki wood handle

6. *Fuguhiki*

The blade of this knife is sleek, thin, and light, designed for slicing *fugu*, or blowfish. Fugu has rather tough elastic white flesh that must be sliced paper-thin to be enjoyed as sashimi.

■ 10.5 inches (270 mm), awase, Yasuki shirogami steel, black water buffalo-horn collar, honoki wood handle (Izutsuki brand)

7. *Kurouchi Ryodeba*

This is a very practical, basic knife: only the cutting edge and the back side are sharpened and polished. The blade is double-ground to handle heavier tasks such as cutting through the thick bones of large fish or chicken.

■ From left: 7.6 inches (195 mm), 7.0 inches (180 mm) and 6.4 inches (165 mm).
Awase, Yasuki *aogami* steel, black water buffalo-horn collar, honoki wood handle (Izutsuki brand)

8. Deba knife

Since fish are a major part of Japanese cuisine, deba come in many lengths. The smallest one is designed for filleting small *aji* horse mackerel, but can be used to fillet any small or thin fish.

■ Far left: 8.4 inches (210 mm), awase, Yasuki shirogami steel, black water buffalo-horn collar, honoki wood handle

Next two, from left: 6.4 inches (165 mm) and 4.8 inches (120 mm).
Awase, Yasuki shirogami steel, black water buffalo-horn collar and honoki wood handle (Izutsuki brand)

9. *Meuchi*, T-shape and straight shape

This is a stiletto-like blade used to pierce an eel's head near the eye to hold it in place for filleting. An *unagi* chef will use the spine or butt of the eel knife to hit the top of the stiletto like an awl. Made of stainless steel.

10. *Unagisaki*, from left: Kyoto-style, Nagoya-style and Osaka-style

Unagi means "eel" and *saki* means "to tear," which refers in this case to filleting. These three Kansai-style eel knives are designed for filleting from the belly. (Compare to the Kanto-style eel knives shown in photo 12.) Made of Yasuki shirogami steel.

11. *Kaimuki*

Kiya makes a few very popular knives for opening shellfish (*kai* refers to shellfish in general; *muki* here means "to shuck"). The knife on the left with the spoon-like head is especially for scallops, whose nearly flat shells are opened as if scraping the inside with the head of the knife. Made of steel.

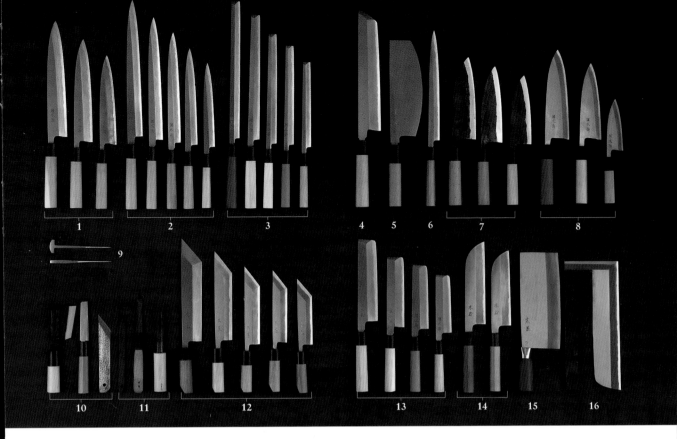

12. Unagisaki, Edo (Tokyo)-style

This Kanto-style eel knife is designed for filleting from the back. The bottom of the handle is beveled and short to allow a firm, slip-free grip when filleting slimy-skinned eels. The larger knife is exclusively for unagi; the smaller ones are used to fillet sea eel and loach.

■ At left: 9.6 inches (240 mm), honyaki, Yasuki shirogami steel, black water buffalo-horn collar, honoki wood handle.
Next four, from left: 8.4 inches (210 mm), 7.0 inches (180 mm), 6.4 inches (165 mm), 6 inches (150 mm), awase, Yasuki shirogami steel. All made of black water buffalo-horn collar and honoki wood handle.

13. Usuba, *higashigata* (Kanto-style)

This Kanto-style usuba is not as popular nowadays as its Kansai-style counterpart, which is curved at the end. The pointed chin is used to cut divots (as when removing the eyes of a potato, for example) and the center section of the blade is used for *katsuramuki* rotary peeling, *ken* needle cutting, beveling, and decorative cuts.

■ From left: 8.4 inches (210 mm), 7.6 inches (190 mm), 7.0 inches (180 mm), 6.4 inches (165 mm) and 6 inches (150 mm).
Awase, Yasuki shirogami steel, black water buffalo-horn collar, honoki wood handle (Izutsuki brand)

14. Usuba, *kamagata* (Kansai-style)

This Kansai-style usuba is widely preferred for cutting vegetables with a broad range of technique; the tip is designed for carving, beveling sharp edges and other detailed tasks. The curve at the end gives the knife greater versatility.

■ 8.4 inches (210 mm) and 7.6 inches (195 mm), awase, Swedish steel, black water buffalo-horn collar and honoki wood handle (with "Shigefusa" insignia)

15. *Chukabocho*

This Chinese cleaver is 4½ inches (110 mm) wide and weighs more than 2 pounds (900 g). Chinese cleavers come in many shapes, depending on the region of China a chef is from. This cleaver has a double-ground edge, making it possible to chop food, cut it into strips, or slice it paper-thin—all with the same tool.

■ 8.8 inches (220 mm), No. 2 (thicker type), Yasuki shirogami steel, stainless-steel bolster and bubinga wood handle

16. *Soba-giri bocho*

The soba-giri is used to cut *soba*, or buckwheat noodles. It has a long, straight cutting edge designed to cut stacked sheets of noodle dough into thin, even strips in the blink of an eye. A wooden handle can be ordered to cover the black part of the handle; some chefs simply wrap it in a towel to get a strong grip. Soba-making is very popular among home chefs in Japan, and Kiya receives numerous orders for custom-made soba knives.

■ 11.7 inches (300 mm), *kurouchi awase*, Yasuki shirogami steel

Knives on Location

Tuna Knives

Filleting tuna, which is a daily task at the Tokyo fish market, takes a great deal of skill and effort. A team of at least three workers is needed, along with an arsenal of tools. In addition to a saw, there is the *maguro bocho*, or tuna knife, a formidably long sword-shaped blade made for filleting these fish that may weigh 440 pounds (200 kg) or more. The blade, around 5 feet in length (150 cm), is used to quarter the entire body cleanly, with two men handling the tool and a third steadying the tuna. Then there's the 40-inch (100 cm) long *hancho*, or half-tool knife, used to make the first cut down to the spine, and later to halve each quarter. There are three smaller knives as well that are used to complete the task, which professionals can carry out in ten minutes.

The maguro bocho are not necessarily of the same quality as Japanese kitchen knives. If the knives were made with a high carbon content, they would chip and crack when working with the large fish. The heavy work of cutting through such large amounts of flesh demands the elasticity of softer steel.

OPPOSITE: The filleting process for this large bluefin takes three men and five knives (including the maguro bocho shown here). Though an experienced team can fillet a tuna in minutes, the job requires tremendous strength and agility; any clumsy mistakes result in lost flesh and profit. "This kind of work—you could do it your whole life and still not be perfect," says Takayuki Shinoda, one of Tokyo's top three tuna wholesalers.

BELOW: The auction hall at Tokyo's fish market, the world's largest. Middlemen walk the rows of tuna, checking each fish and deciding which to bid on. An expert eye can assess the flavor and texture of the tuna by examining the flesh at the belly cut and the point where the tail is severed.

Unagi knives

Regional differences in the preparation of eel are reflected in the types of knives used in each area: Tokyo, Nagoya, Kyoto, Osaka, and Kyushu all have their own types of *unagi-bocho*. *Unagi* is generally filleted butterfly-style, but chefs in the area around Tokyo fillet them from the back, while those in the Kyoto-Osaka area, and nearly everywhere else in Japan, fillet them from the belly. Preparation varies between the regions as well: In the Tokyo area eel fillets are steamed before grilling, but around Kyoto and Osaka they are grilled straight away.

Eels are kept alive until the last minute before filleting, when they are put in a bucket of ice water to slow them down. When the eel is put on the cutting board, a stiletto-like *meuchi* is used to pierce its head and pin it down to the board. A decisive, straight cut with the heel of the knife kills the eel instantly; the chef then zips the heavy, angular unagi-bocho down the length of the eel's body, filleting it butterfly-style. A professional unagi chef can fillet three eels in two minutes.

A live eel is pinned to the board with the *meuchi* and killed with a straight cut behind the head, then expertly filleted in less than a minute.

Nodaiwa is one of Tokyo's most famous *unagi* restaurants. They take particular care to select the best wild-caught eels and follow an exacting preparation process that includes grilling over charcoal, steaming, and grilling again while basting with a sweet *tare* sauce. Nodaiwa's chefs fillet as many as five hundred eels in a single day.

The tools of the trade: the *meuchi* and the *unagi-bocho*. The Kanto-style knife shown here is designed for splitting eels from the back. The wide, straight tip of the blade is double-ground to keep the knife from hitting the eel's central nerve. The point where the angled tip meets the main edge is used to remove the gills.

The *soba-giri bocho* is an impressive block of steel between 10 and 14½ inches (24 and 36 cm) in length, 4 inches (10 cm) in height and weighing more than 2 pounds (about a kilogram). To facilitate cutting through the soft dough in a single downward stroke, the knife is designed with the handle near the center.

Matsuya-Kanda's famous hand-cut *soba* noodles. Without the soba-giri bocho, cutting noodles so uniformly thin would be an impossible task. Unfortunately, soba shops that make their noodles entirely by hand are increasingly rare.

OPPOSITE: Takayuki Kodaka, head chef at Matsuya-Kanda, cutting *soba* noodles. A wooden guide, or *komaita*, held in the left hand, helps keep the width of the cuts uniform. The knife handle is covered with sharkskin, which helps Kodaka to maintain a steady grip when wielding this heavy knife.

Soba knife

Buckwheat, or *soba*, has been cultivated in Japan for more than a thousand years. Noodles made from buckwheat became popular some three hundred years ago, when laborers crowded the booming city of Edo. They loved the refreshing, slightly sweet flavor and energy-boosting properties of these noodles—not to mention the speed with which they could be eaten. Soba is Japan's original fast food, and soba shops still outnumber hamburger chain outlets.

At Matsuya-Kanda, one such soba shop in Tokyo, the noodle dough is made from buckwheat flour, with some wheat flour added for elasticity (eggs are used as a binder). A cypress-wood pole is used to roll and stretch the dough into a paper-thin sheet that is folded into an eight-layer stack for cutting. The heavy *soba-giri bocho* essentially shaves away ⅛-inch (3 mm) strips from the stack to create a bundle of long, perfect noodles. Matsuya's simple *zaru* soba, cooked noodles served on a lacquered tray accompanied by a cup of dipping sauce, is the perfect way to savor the delicate sweetness of fresh soba noodles.

Hamo knife

Hamo, or daggertooth pike conger, is only in season from June to the end of August. A classic menu item in summer, it is often enjoyed as sashimi or tempura, or in *shabu-shabu*.

This long, thick-skinned fish, which belongs to the eel family, has innumerable hard bones that must be cut and softened before cooking so that the fish can be eaten with ease. This process, called *hamo no honekiri* (literally "conger-bone cutting"), cuts and separates the bones. The fish is first filleted butterfly-style with a *deba* knife, and the skin left on. The chef then uses the long, thin *hamokiri* (conger knife) to make a series of vertical cuts at close intervals, working from the left and going all the way down the fillet. When the process is finished, the fillet may be cut into 1-inch (2.4 cm) pieces and blanched to soften the skin before being served as sashimi.

The long, straight-tipped hamokiri has a thick spine. The weight of the blade, rather than the chef's strength, is used to cut through the rows of hard bones all the way down to—but not into or through—the thick skin. Chefs must cut the *hamo* fillet at very close intervals (above right), about 20 cuts per inch (8 cuts per centimeter).

133

Maintenance and More

SHARPENING

The Stone

A carbon-steel Japanese knife should never be sharpened with anything other than a water stone, since using a sharpening steel or an oilstone would ruin the cutting edge. Professionals use three different grades of water stone to sharpen their knives: the *arato* (coarse stone), the *nakato* (fine stone) and the *shiageto* (finishing or extra-fine stone). For the home cook, the nakato stone will suffice.

Although natural water stones are still found in Japan, especially in Kyoto and Kumamoto prefectures, their increasing rarity has made them expensive—as much as a thousand dollars for a single stone. These days, they are mainly used for polishing traditional Japanese swords; most people use synthetic water stones—usually aluminum or silicon carbide—for maintaining cooking knives. These are inexpensive and more readily available than natural water stones, in addition to being easier to use.

Both natural and synthetic water stones come in a range of grain sizes, from as coarse as 80 to as fine as 8,000 grit. To determine the grit of a water stone, the abrasive grains are passed through a sieve. The number of holes in the sieve within a one-inch (2.5 cm) square corresponds to the number of the grit. Therefore, a #800 (800 grit) *arato* coarse stone consists of grains that passed through an 800-hole-per-inch sieve. Since a greater number of holes per inch means that the holes are smaller, higher numbers indicate a finer grit.

Synthetic stones are categorized just like the natural stones. The coarse arato ranges from 80 to 220 grit, and is mostly used on newly purchased knives that have not yet been sharpened. The fine nakato ranges from 400 to 1500 grit, and is considered the basic stone for sharpening, with a wider range of uses than the other two. The extra-fine shiageto generally has a grain of more than 3000 grit, and sharpens knives very finely. It does the subtle work of finishing uneven surface areas, and makes the edge razor-sharp.

The beautifully-grained stone on the left is a natural water stone used by an artisan in Sakai who specializes in sharpening knives. On the right is a synthetic stone. Synthetic water stones are the best choice for everyday use in sharpening kitchen knives.

Knife makers and retailers, as well as professional chefs, generally agree that the fine-grit nakato is the only stone the home chef needs. In Japan, most knife shops will gladly sharpen a new knife after it is purchased, and will also hone or repair chips on a damaged blade. Online knife retailers vary in the services they offer. When purchasing a knife online, it is wise to compare sellers to see which ones offer this service.

Maintaining the Stone

Water stones need regular maintenance, just like knives. The flat surface of the stone will become uneven with use, making it difficult to sharpen a blade evenly. In this case, a "fixer" stone, which is harder than the water stone, is required. The fixer stone is placed on top of the uneven stone and rubbed back and forth along the length of the water stone until both faces meet flat against one another. In a pinch, a brick can be used for this purpose, though it is not recommended for resurfacing the fine shiageto. Of course, any Japanese knife store should be able to restore the surface of a water stone as well.

The Sharpening Process

Before sharpening, the stone must be soaked in water for about thirty minutes. A dry stone is far too rough to allow even and smooth sharpening, and simply wetting the surface is not sufficient—the stone will soak up the water like a dry sponge and will remain too dry to sharpen effectively. The surface of the stone should also be sprinkled with water whenever it begins to dry out during the sharpening process. But it is crucial not to wash away the *toguso*, the gritty slurry produced during sharpening. This acts as a sharpening agent on its own.

Sharpening a single-ground knife is not difficult. The principal difference between a Japanese knife and a Western knife is that the area that lies against the stone, called the *kiriba* blade path, is wider in Japanese knives [illustration 1 on the following page]. In sharpening, the kiriba blade path should remain uniform in width from tip to heel [illustration 2]. The shinogi acts as a guide, showing the line to follow in sharpening the knife. For example, the usuba has a straight shinogi and cutting edge, so the knife moves straight up and down the stone as it is sharpened. The shinogi of the deba and yanagiba curves toward the tip, as does the cutting edge. Therefore, when sharpening the curved section of these knives, the blade

follows an arc from the bottom of the stone to the top (see details on page 139). The knife should always follow the shinogi line as it moves across the sharpening stone.

When the *omote* (edge side) is correctly sharpened, a *kaeri* or long regular burr is formed [illustration 3] toward the *ura* (back side) of the blade. The kaeri may be visible as a white line down the edge because it reflects the light. It can also be felt when the blade is touched lightly with the cushion of the left thumb. The process of sharpening the knife actually consists of repeatedly forming and removing kaeri.

Although it looks straight to the naked eye, a sharpened edge appears jagged, like a saw, if viewed under magnification. A knife uses notches to cut, just like a saw, but on a much finer level; this is why a Japanese knife cuts best when it is pulled. The extra-fine shiageto stone is used as a final step to make the notches as fine as possible, since the finer the notches, the better the knife will cut. (Incidentally, the shiageto should only be used on carbon steel, not stainless steel. On a stainless steel knife, the shiageto will make such fine notches that they no longer catch the material being cut, and the blade will be ineffective.)

Some professionals put a double edge [illustration 4] on the blade. The second cutting edge is called the *koba*, and while it does not affect the sharpness, it does greatly improve the durability. Some chefs prefer having a koba on the lower part of the deba blade, where it can be used for tougher chores like chopping bones. A koba can be easily made by moving the blade at a more acute angle during the finishing-stone stage [illustration 5]. The *kaeri* is then removed by sharpening the back side.

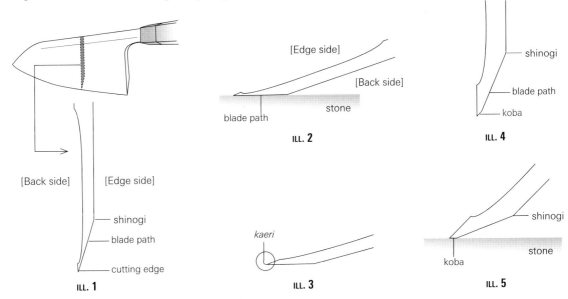

[Edge side]

[Back side]

blade path

stone

ILL. 2

shinogi

blade path

koba

ILL. 4

[Back side]   [Edge side]

shinogi

blade path

cutting edge

ILL. 1

kaeri

ILL. 3

shinogi

stone

koba

ILL. 5

Sharpening the *usuba* knife

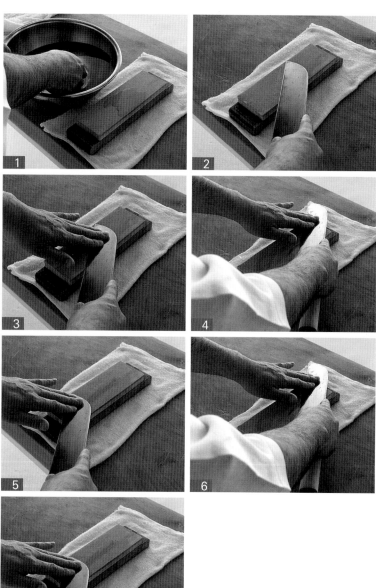

1. Have a bowl of water ready nearby, or work near the sink, to be able to easily moisten the stone during sharpening. Place the soaked stone on a damp towel to keep it in place.

2. Hold the knife in the right hand, with the index finger on the spine and the thumb near the heel. Place the knife near the bottom of the stone, on a diagonal between four and five o'clock. Sharpen the blade in sections, not all at once. Start with the upper third of the edge (tip end).

3. Place the three middle fingers of the hand on the area to be sharpened. The angle of the knife edge to the stone depends on the knife, but in general, the highest point between the stone and the blade should be about the height of two small coins stacked on top of each other.

4, 5. Pressing gently with the left fingers, move the blade straight up the length of the stone. Release the pressure completely and move the knife back down to the bottom of the stone. The sharpening action takes place as the knife moves upward, not downward.

6, 7. Repeat 4 and 5 using fast, rhythmic motions, stopping occasionally to moisten the stone and to test the edge.

When touching the sharpened edge with the pad of the left thumb, you should feel a slight drag or catch as the *kaeri*, or burr, grabs your skin a little. This ensures the knife has been sharpened correctly.

8, 9. When the kaeri on the first section of the edge side of the knife has formed, repeat the process for the next section. Move all the way down the knife to the heel.

10. Now work on the back side of the blade. Turn the knife so that the edge is away from you. The right index finger should be placed near the neck. Keep the thumb on the spine. With the left fingers on the flat of the blade, move the knife upward with pressure and downward without in the same manner as before. The edge side should be sharpened 70%, and the back side should be sharpened 30%. The main purpose of working on the back side is to remove the kaeri that formed while working on the edge side. As before, sharpen each section of the blade from tip to heel. Stop from time to time to sprinkle water on the stone and to test the edge.

11. Approaching the heel, the handle of the knife will get in the way. Move the knife so it is nearly perpendicular to the stone.

When the kaeri forms on this side, turn the knife to work on the edge side and remove the kaeri. Work down the length of the blade on both sides (keeping in mind that 70% of the sharpening takes place on the edge side) until the knife is sharp enough.

Drop a little water from your hand to the stone to keep the sharpening process smooth, but don't wash away the slurry that forms as you work. The slurry, called *toguso,* is an important sharpening agent.

Sharpening the *deba* or *yanagiba* knife

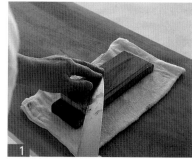

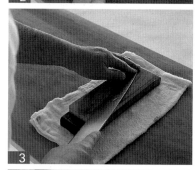

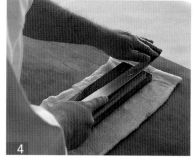

Knives that have a curved tip, like the deba or yanagiba, require extra care when sharpening so that the curve is maintained.

When sharpening the curved tip of a deba or yanagi knife, the blade should move in an arc from the lower left to the upper center of the stone. Begin with the blade on a diagonal; when the stroke is finished, the knife should be vertical (parallel to the length of the stone). Moving the blade across the stone in an arc will maintain its curved edge.

Repeat on the back side of the blade, continuing to sharpen as above.

DAILY MAINTENANCE

Handling and Cleaning

Carbon-steel knives should always be kept dry to prevent rusting. After use, wash the knife, wipe away the water with a soft cloth, and leave the knife to air-dry. Pouring hot water over the blade will speed air-drying. Never heat the knife over a flame, as this will weaken the hardened carbon steel. To remove stubborn stains near the spine and on the back of the knife, use a wine cork and fine-grain powdered cleanser. (Some chefs use thick *daikon* radish ends instead of cork.) Rinse away the cleanser completely, then dry and sharpen the knife. Do not try to remove stains near the knife edge by rubbing with the cork; it is too easy to slip and cut a finger.

Carbon steel should not be exposed to acidic food for any length of time. When cutting acidic foods like lemons or tomatoes, try to wipe or wash the knife frequently. It's a good idea to keep a damp folded cloth close at hand to wipe the blade when working.

If the knife is not used on a daily basis, it should always be washed, wiped and air-dried completely after using. Put a little vegetable oil on a paper towel and lightly coat the dry knife with oil. Finally, wrap the knife with the newspaper or put it in its *saya* wooden sheath and store it. Before using a stored knife, wash it with detergent and dry it well.

To prevent the knife from chipping, never use it to cut frozen items, and avoid putting excessive pressure on the blade. Each type of knife should be used only for its intended purpose—for example, a *yanagiba* should never be used to cut through thick bones. In addition, when not using the knife, never leave it in a position near the edge of the counter or work surface where it can fall any distance. The knife should rest with the blade facing away, parallel to the side of the cutting board, either in the center of the board or in a safe place beyond it.

Repairing a Damaged Blade

Removal of chips and rust damage should be left to knife professionals. However, if there are no other options, it is possible to salvage a chipped or rusted knife with an *arato* coarse stone. For chips, use the arato to hone away the entire cutting edge in a straight line until the chip disappears completely [illustrations 6 and 7]. Next, sharpen the face and back with the arato, removing the *kaeri* burr each time. The larger the chip, the narrower the edge will become after the chip is removed [illustration 8]. In order to maintain the width of the edge, the *shinogi* ridge line must be raised. Use the arato coarse stone to widen the edge, making sure to keep the shinogi line parallel to the *hado* blade path [illustration 9]. Finally, use a *nakato* fine stone for finishing. A *shiageto* fine stone can be used to finish the job. For rust damage, the procedure is the same as for chips: hone away the edge until the rusted part is gone.

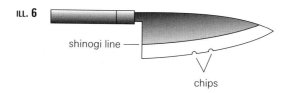

ILL. **6**

shinogi line —

chips

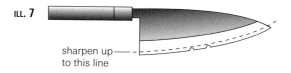

ILL. **7**

sharpen up — to this line

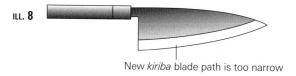

ILL. **8**

New *kiriba* blade path is too narrow

How many times can a knife be sharpened? With steel-jacketed *awase* knives, the chips or rusts can be honed away until the *hagane* steel on the back side, which makes up the cutting edge, is worn away. The soft iron core of the blade cannot be made into a cutting edge. With single-forged *honyaki* knives, the chips or rusts can be honed away until the tempered steel (delineated by the waved temper line) is worn away. Untempered steel cannot be sharpened into a cutting edge.

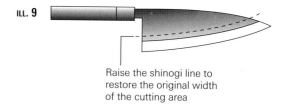

ILL. **9**

Raise the shinogi line to restore the original width of the cutting area

143

PURCHASING A JAPANESE KNIFE

Making a Choice

The most suitable type of knife really depends on the cook. Most home cooks in Japan have an *usuba* (also called a *nakiri-bocho*) and a *deba*. An all-purpose double-ground knife called a *santoku* is also found in many kitchens; the *gyuto*, or beef slicer, which is versatile enough to cut many things, is another popular choice. Those who enjoy cooking and frequently hold parties at home generally have a few more specialized knives. For example, they may have a good *yanagiba* if they like slicing sashimi out of fish fillets from the supermarket. Cooks who are serious about Japanese cuisine should have an usuba and a deba at minimum.

For casual cooks, as well as those who do not have experience with Japanese knives, an awase knife is a better choice than a honyaki blade. Even if the carbon steel edge of an awase knife is chipped or cracked, the damage will be minimal because the softer upper part of the knife will stay intact. Furthermore, an awase blade is far easier to sharpen.

FROM THE LEFT:

Nakiri, 6.4 in. (165 mm), SK-4 steel, with *honoki* wood handle and black water buffalo collar (Seki Magoroku / Kai)

Tokujo santoku, 7.0 in. (180 mm), V1 steel with laminated wood handle (Tsukiji Masamoto)

Deba, 6.4 in. (165 mm), VG-10 super steel, with pakkawood handle (Shun Pro Series / Kai)

Banno (all-purpose) deba, 6 in. (150 mm), high carbon special steel, with a *karin* quince-wood handle (Nenox S1 / Nenohi)

A master sharpener working on a customer's blade at a knife shop near the Tsukiji market

Those who are well versed in using an awase knife might be ready to consider a honyaki blade. Honyaki knives are much more expensive since they are forged at an artisanal level; they cannot be mass-produced. Because of the forging process they hold an edge longer than awase knives. For people who cook professionally with a single purpose such as cutting sashimi all day, a honyaki knife is the best choice.

Both awase and honyaki knives are made from standard carbon steel and therefore rust easily. However, single-ground knives made of new types of rust-resistant carbon steel can be found. Single-ground knives made of stainless steel for ease of use are also available.

Traditional Japanese knives are ground only on the right side, and are intended for right-handed use. Left-handed knives are not hard to find, but they are generally not as widely available. They can be custom-ordered as well.

Where to Buy

If possible, it is best to purchase a knife at a local outlet. This makes it possible to ensure that the knife is not warped, that its balance is suitable, and that it has no surface scratches or blemishes. Because most single-ground Japanese knives are hand forged, they are naturally all slightly different. These differences are very subtle, but it is very important to find the knife that feels best when actually held in the hand. Even for those who don't know much about knives, letting "what feels good" guide the knife purchase is a sound course of action. If buying online is the only option, make sure the seller offers certain maintenance services, including *honba-tsuke* (explained below), sharpening, and repairing serious rusting, chips and cracks.

When buying a knife, it is a good idea to purchase at least a *nakato* water stone at the same time, as well as a good wooden cutting board. Wooden cutting boards are preferable to plastic, as carbon steel knives work better on softer surfaces.

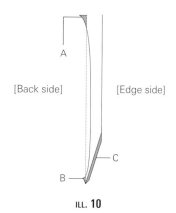

[Back side]   [Edge side]

A

C

B

ILL. **10**

Honba-tsuke Service

Japanese knives are often sold as shown in illustration 10, with the gray area from A to C needing to be removed. The removal of this area is called

145

honba-tsuke, "making a real edge." The process of removing the area between A and B is called *ura-oshi*, or flattening the back side. Honba-tsuke service is common in Japan, whether the blade comes from a knife shop or via the Internet, but it may be difficult to find someone with these skills in a local knife shop outside Japan. Some knives are sold with honba-tsuke already completed; again, it is best to confirm this with the seller before buying a knife.

Knives for Collectors

Honyaki *yanagiba* knives have become something of a collector's item around the world because of their sword-like shape, the sleek appeal of their surface, and the beautiful wave pattern created in forging. In Japan, yanagiba and *soba* knives are the styles most frequently custom-ordered by collectors. Mirror-finished knives have also become very popular in Japan recently, especially for *yanagiba*, since these long knives showcase the mirror finish beautifully. The glossy mirror surface is created on ordinary knives by polishing them with special fine-grain compounds; these can be purchased through the Internet.

Suminagashi knives (see page 24) got their name from a drawing technique in which a sheet of paper is placed on a dish of water where a little oil-based ink is floating, creating a beautiful marbling pattern on the paper. For suminagashi blades, layers of the soft iron and steel are forge-welded, hammered and polished. The alternating layers take on a pattern similar to suminagashi paper.

Western-style Damascus blades are forged in a manner somewhat similar to the suminagashi technique. The name came from a folded-steel forging method probably invented in Persia and introduced to Europe through the Syrian city of Damascus. The exact method has been lost to history, but knife companies today use a variety of techniques to re-create the appearance of Damascus-forged steel. Damascus and suminagashi knives are sometimes incorrectly referred to as *kasumi*, a term that refers to knives forged by the *awase* method. Terminology aside, suminagashi and Damascus cladding are cosmetic enhancements and will not affect the performance of the knife.

Right-handed *kamagata* usuba, 7.6 in.(195 mm). Awase, Swedish steel, with a *honoki* wooden handle and black water buffalo-horn collar (Shigefusa / Kiya)

ON RIGHT (THREE KNIVES):
Left-handed *higashigata* usuba 6.4 in. (165 mm), left-handed yanagiba 9.6 in. (240 mm), left-handed deba 6.4 in. (165 mm). All awase, and made of shirogami steel with honoki wood handles and black water buffalo-horn collars (Yoshihisa / Kiya)

JAPANESE KNIFE MATERIALS

The Blade

The materials used to make Japanese knives can be grouped into two categories. One is carbon steel, a material used in most Japanese knives. Carbon steel is made in the forge by adding carbon to steel made from iron sand. *Honyaki* knives are made completely of carbon steel, while *awase* (*kasumi*) knives are made by combining carbon steel and softer iron.

The second category of materials includes stainless steel. To make stainless steel, chrome (more than 12%) is added to carbon steel. Because this prevents rusting, stainless steel is used in both Japanese and Western knives made for home use.

Japanese kitchen knives used to be forged from *tamahagane* Japan steel, which is a carbon steel made using the ancient *tatara* blast furnace method. However, these days the main material is Yasuki Specialty Steel (YSS). YSS, which has a high carbon content, was invented by Hitachi Metals Ltd. using the ideas behind tatara blast-furnace methods to create steel that could be mass-produced. YSS, considered to be the top quality steel for forging today's Japanese kitchen knives, comes in several different varieties, depending on the percentage of the metals and other materials. These are named using colors, e.g., *shirogami* ("white-paper"), or *aogami* ("blue-paper"). (Originally, the varieties of YSS were differentiated by pasting paper labels of various colors on the steel.)

JIS SK steel

Contains carbon, as well as impurities such as phosphorus and sulfur. JIS SK steel is used for hand tools such as saws and axes.

YSS *kigami* (yellow-paper)

This carbon steel contains fewer impurities than SK steel. It is used for high-quality hand tools and in low-quality kitchen knives for home use.

YSS *shirogami* (white-paper)

With impurities reduced even further, this is the purest type of YSS carbon steel, and the closest to *tamahagane* Japan steel. It is also used as a base for developing additional varieties of YSS. Forging shirogami steel is extremely difficult. Since very few artisans can forge kitchen knives with this material, shirogami knives are rare. This type of steel tends to rust easily, but some say that it cuts better than any other steel.

YSS *aogami* (blue-paper)

This is shirogami (white-paper) steel with chrome and tungsten added. Aogami is the most popular steel for forging high-quality kitchen knives.

YSS aogami "super"

This steel is made by adding molybdenum and vanadium, along with additional chrome and tungsten, to aogami (blue-paper) steel. It contains 1.4–1.5% carbon.

YSS *gingami* (silver-paper)

This type of stainless steel is created by adding chrome (more than 13%) to shirogami (white-paper) steel.

Swedish steel

This is a very pure carbon steel made in Sweden. Misono, a Japanese knife-maker, uses this high-quality steel for one of its knife series. If improperly maintained, Swedish steel rusts just as YSS carbon steel does, but it holds an edge well and cuts food very cleanly.

Since a higher carbon content makes a harder, sharper blade, professionals prefer high-carbon YSS steel to stainless steel. However, the high percentage of carbon makes these knives easy to damage and difficult to sharpen, so stainless steel knives are popular among casual cooks. Nowadays, many steel companies are working to develop new kinds of high-quality and well-balanced steel by adding other components to the carbon steel. These new varieties of steel are often named after the company that produced them or the materials that were added.

The Handle and the Collar

Wood from the *honoki* tree, a species of magnolia, is used to make the handle for a traditional Japanese knife. A honoki wood handle provides a firm grip to prevent slipping, and is smooth and comfortable in the hand. Some knives have handles made of *kokutan* ebony or *keyaki* Japanese zelkova wood. Whatever the material, the wooden handle is attached by heating the *nakago* or tang of the knife (see knife anatomy on page 17) and inserting it into a hole drilled into the wood by pounding the bottom of the handle. As the nakago cools, the wood of the handle shrinks around it, making it perfectly secure without glue or bolts. The wooden handle may eventually become worn, or the tang may rust inside if the knife is improperly maintained. If this happens, the knife should be sent back to the store for a replacement handle.

The water buffalo-horn collar, called the *kakumaki*, is attached to keep the wood of the handle from cracking when the nakago tang is heated and driven firmly into the handle of the knife by pounding the bottom with a mallet. Though traditionally made of water buffalo-horn, inexpensive plastic collars are sometimes used as well.

The *Saya* Wooden Sheath

The *saya* wooden sheath for a knife is often sold separately. Saya are generally made of the same wood as the handle of the knife they hold (*honoki* wood in most cases). Saya should be ideally purchased or ordered when purchasing a knife, since they may require slight adjustments to keep the knife snug in the sheath. For knife collectors, a saya is indispensable, as it is generally displayed alongside the knife. If a knife is used on a regular basis for cooking, however, a saya is unnecessary.

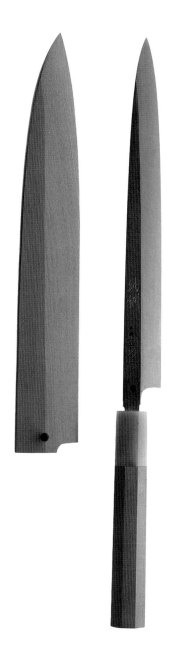

Yanagiba, 9.6 in. (240 mm). Honyaki, shirogami steel, with *honoki* wood handle and white water buffalo-horn collar. The saya is also made of honoki wood. (Tsukiji Masamoto)

FISH ANATOMY

Understanding fish anatomy is invaluable for cleaning and filleting processes.

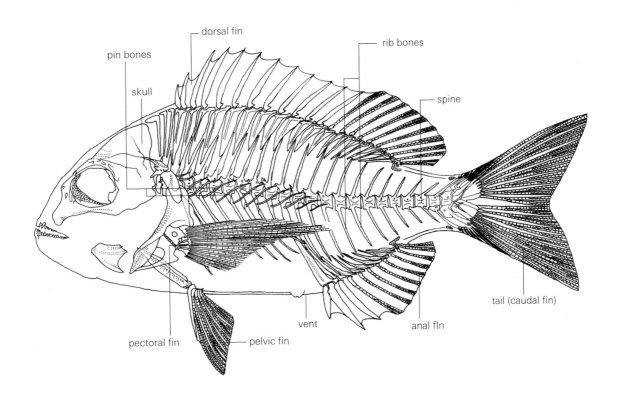

MOVEMENT OF THE BLADE

This illustration shows the progress of the cutting edge of the knife toward the spine of the fish during filleting. The filleting is not done with a single stroke, but by making several passes across the bones, adjusting the angle of the cutting edge to match the angle of the bones.

GLOSSARY

Aji

Japanese horse mackerel, *Tracherus japonicus*. This small (8 in. / 20 cm) fish resembles a mackerel, but is actually a member of the jack family. There are two types of aji, the yellowish inshore variety and the darker, longer-bodied offshore type. Aji is one of the most common food fish in Japan.

Ankimo

This word refers to the liver of the monkfish, *Lophius piscatorius*. Creamy and rich, steamed ankimo is a traditional winter delicacy in Japan.

Ayu

Sweetfish, *Plecoglossis altivelis*. This trout-like freshwater fish averages 6 inches (15 cm) in length. In certain places ayu is fished using trained cormorants. Prized for its sweet flesh, it is often enjoyed grilled with salt from early summer to fall.

Daikon radish

This long, white, mild-fleshed variety of radish is a mainstay of Japanese cooking. Served raw, it can be ground, shredded *ken*-style, or sliced into thin sheets *katsuramuki*-style. It is also often sliced into thick rounds, beveled and simmered in many different dishes. In addition, daikon is commonly pickled with rice bran, salt, or vinegar. The part furthest from the stem has a sharper flavor; daikon is also sweeter in winter.

Dashi

A cornerstone of Japanese cuisine, dashi is stock or broth with a *kombu* kelp base. The most common type of dashi is made with kombu and *katsuobushi* bonito flakes, but dried shiitake mushrooms and dried baby sardines, along with other dried fish, may also be used.

Engawa

The engawa is the ridged section of muscle along the border of a flatfish fillet. It is considered the best part of the fish to use for sashimi because of its slightly crunchy texture.

Fugu

Japanese blowfish (puffer fish), *Fugu rubripes*. As the ovaries, skin, muscle, and especially the liver of this fish contain lethal tetrodoxin, which is similar to curare, it must be dressed by certified professionals. The mild, elastic flesh is sliced paper-thin and eaten as sashimi; it may also be eaten grilled, deep-fried, or simmered in nabe. Fugu is one of the most expensive foods in Japan.

Gobo

Greater burdock root. This long, hairy root is a Japanese staple. It has a sweet, slightly earthy flavor and a fibrous texture. Place it in water after cutting to prevent discoloration and to reduce the harshness of its flavor. Gobo is used in many dishes, but most popularly in *kimpira gobo*, julienned gobo and carrot sautéed in sesame oil and seasoned with soy sauce, red chili pepper, sugar, and mirin or sake.

Hirame

Fluke or summer flounder, *Paralichthys dentatus*. With its mild, slightly sweet flavor and delicate texture, fluke is one of the most popular white-fleshed fish used for sushi.

Hocho

This is the generic Japanese word for "kitchen knife." The names of different types of knives generally end in the suffix -hocho or -bocho, e.g., *deba-bocho* filleting knife.

Iwashi

Sardine, *Sardinops sagax*. This small fish, a member of the herring family, has a full flavor and rich flesh. Iwashi are generally caught at about 8 inches (20 cm) long, and are often served as sushi or sashimi with a dab of grated ginger and sliced green onions on top.

Josei

This term means "superior" and can be used interchangeably with *tokujo*.

Kabayaki

See Unagi.

Kansai

The area of western Japan centered around Osaka, and including Kyoto and Kobe.

Kanto
The area of eastern Japan centered around Tokyo.

Katsuo
Skipjack tuna (bonito), *Katsuwonus pelamis*. Most commonly smoked, dried into blocks, and finely shaved to make *katsuobushi* bonito flakes, katsuo also is wonderful eaten in season (summer and early autumn) as sashimi. It is often served *tataki*-style, briefly seared on the outside, with grated garlic, raw onion, grated ginger, *momiji-oroshi* ground daikon and red pepper, or citrusy *ponzu* sauce.

Kimpira
See Gobo.

Kombu
Kombu, a seaweed from the genus *Laminaria*, is an important part of Japanese cuisine. Rich in glutamic acid, it lends umami to any dish. Kombu is usually dried before use, but it may also be pickled or eaten fresh.

Kyuri
Japanese cucumber. These thin-skinned, spiny cucumbers are long and slender, with tiny seeds. If kyuri are not available, seeded common cucumbers are a fine substitute.

Mentaiko
Mentaiko is brined cod or pollock roe; it is often spiced with red peppers. Spicy mentaiko is popularly eaten on spaghetti, but it is also delicious on hot rice. Many find its salty, spicy flavor addictive.

Mirin
This sweet rice wine is an essential kitchen ingredient. Be sure to buy "hon-mirin," which actually contains wine made from rice. Some mirin varieties are sold with additive sweeteners such as dextrose; these are best avoided.

Naganegi
Long onion. This variety of scallion, sold commonly in Japan but difficult to find in the West, is about two feet (60 cm) long and an inch (2.5 cm) thick. Naganegi has a mild onion flavor and becomes wonderfully sweet when cooked. Leeks can be substituted for naganegi in recipes where they are cooked; for a raw substitute, the smaller Western green onions work well.

Nasu
Japanese eggplant. These are far smaller and more elongated than their Western cousins. They have thin skin, fine-textured flesh, and tiny seeds. A summer favorite, there are myriad ways of preparing nasu: grilling, braising, frying, steaming, and pickling, to name only a few.

Nijimasu
Rainbow trout, *Oncorhynchus mykiss*. These freshwater fish are not native to Japan, but were imported in the nineteenth century. They thrive in Japan's rivers and are a popular catch in fly fishing.

Nori
These purplish square sheets of pounded laver turn bright green when roasted. Best known as the wrapping around rolled sushi and *onigiri* rice balls, nori can be scissored into thin strips and used to top noodles or hot rice. Roasted nori quickly turns limp and stale, and should be kept in an airtight tin.

Otoshi-buta
A circular wooden drop-lid, slightly smaller in circumference than the pot it is used with. The otoshi-buta floats on top of simmered dishes, ensuring that the heat is evenly distributed and keeping the ingredients from boiling too hard. The otoshi-buta should be soaked in water for a few minutes prior to using so that it does not absorb flavors.

Rice vinegar
Vinegar made with rice is mild and mellow. Several kinds of rice vinegars are available, including brown rice vinegar and seasoned rice vinegar, which is sweetened for use in sushi rice. Be careful when purchasing, as it is easy to get the wrong one. For recipes in this book, plain rice vinegar is best.

Saba
Mackerel, *Scomber scombrus*. Saba is an important food fish in Japan because of its relative abundance. Though many in the West dislike its strong flavor, it is a favorite in Japan, particularly grilled, or marinated in vinegar and served as sashimi. It tastes best in fall, when its high fat content gives it an even richer taste. It should be eaten as fresh as possible.

Sawara
Spanish mackerel, *Scomberomorus niphonia*. These medium-sized (30 inch / 80 cm) fish are one of Japan's most popular food fish. Sawara is often sliced for sashimi or sushi, grilled, or simmered. It is at its peak in winter.

Shiso
Also known as Japanese basil, or beefsteak plant, shiso is an important herb in Japan. Not only its fragrant leaves, but its buds and tiny purple flowers as well, are used to enhance sashimi as a garnish. It is also a key ingredient in certain kinds of pickles. Shiso leaves have a distinctive, delicate flavor. They are delicious chiffonaded and put in a salad, omelet or stir-fry.

Sunomono

In Japanese cuisine, this word refers to salad-like dishes prepared with vinegar. Sunomono often contain seaweed, and are generally slightly sweet, complementing the mild tartness of rice vinegar. They are a great appetizer, and also work well to refresh the palate between courses.

Tai

Sea bream, *Pagrus major*. This handsome red-striped fish is considered a good-luck symbol in Japan, and is therefore served on auspicious occasions. It is one of the most popular fish in Japanese cuisine. Tai is best eaten in winter or early spring.

Takezaru

A type of bamboo sieve used to drain noodles and serve food.

Tokujo

This term means "superior," and can be used interchangeably with *josei*.

Tsuma

Tsuma is the generic name for any of the many kinds of fresh vegetable garnishes used to enhance the presentation of sashimi. The most common of these is *ken*-cut daikon, but various kinds of seaweed and leafy vegetables are also used.

Umami

Umami is now accepted as one of the five basic tastes (in addition to sour, sweet, salty, and bitter). Foods rich in umami—commonly fermented or aged foods—contain glutamic acid or glutamates that lend a savory, hearty flavor.

Unagi

Japanese freshwater eel, *Anguilla japonica*. Unagi is most often served as *kabayaki*, barbecued eel: fillets of unagi are steamed, then grilled over charcoal and basted with a sweet *tare* sauce. They may be eaten as-is, or laid over steamed rice (*una-don*). *Anago*, the sea-going counterpart of unagi, has a slightly less fatty texture and subtler flavor.

Yuzu

This citrus fruit, native to East Asia, has a haunting fragrance and sour flesh. It is rarely eaten out of hand; the rind is used as a garnish and flavoring agent. Yuzu marmalade is a treat as well.

Wasabi

This relative of horseradish grows only in clear, cold, mountain streams. Though the fresh-ground root is incomparable for its sweet pungency, wasabi can also be bought in tubes, or in powdered form (these contain many other ingredients besides wasabi, including horseradish, flour, and coloring). To reconstitute, place about two teaspoons in a small cup and add ice-cold water a little at a time, using a chopstick to stir rapidly, until it becomes a soft paste. Invert the cup over a saucer to prevent the flavor from evaporating. If fresh wasabi root is available, an *oroshi* sharkskin grater is the best tool to use to grind it into paste.

Zuwai-gani

Snow crab, *Chionoecetes opilio*. In season during the winter months, this is a sought-after and expensive delicacy in Japan.

AFTERWORD

My first Japanese kitchen knife was a Misono "petty," a thin version of the paring knife. The first time I used it—to slice through a tomato—was a revelation, so swift and clean was the action. A few years later, in the midst of researching a book on Japanese cooking tools, I got my hands on the three main types of knives, the *deba*, *usuba* and *yanagiba*. But the truth is I only owned the knives, but had yet to "earn" them. In fact, I had little confidence in using my specialist knives for their intended purposes.

There are many publications on knife usage in Japanese, but they tend to assume readers already have a certain level of experience. Hiromitsu Nozaki of Tokyo's famed Waketokuyama restaurant is not only an extraordinary chef, he is also a born teacher. In his many writings, lectures, and classes, he uses simple language to explain nutrition, food culture, and cooking. So I asked if he might be interested in working on a book in English to illuminate the complex world of Japanese kitchen knives. Luckily, he agreed.

Over the course of nearly a year, Nozaki and his comradely team of apprentice chefs went out of their way to show me the whys of their world, starting with posture. Once Nozaki positioned me in the correct way, the knife truly became an extension of my arm and cutting ingredients became almost effortless. He also guided my hands with his, showing me how to feed and rotate the daikon into the usuba for rotary peeling, for example, or how to tap the deba handle against a crab claw to see it break away.

Toward the end of our project Nozaki gave me an entire sea bream to take home to gut, fillet in five pieces, and slice into sashimi. I was terrified. But I pulled out my scaler, yanagiba and deba, put the beast into the sink and jumped into the messy work of scaling. It was to be a rocky journey with some pretty sloppy work. But I was rewarded with a feast, where every bit of the fish was used. I was at least beginning to earn my knives.

I hope you enjoy this chance to learn cutting techniques from the chef's perspective, and that, like me, you discover just how exciting it can be to work with a sharp *hocho*, fresh ingredients, and the right methods.

Kate Klippensteen

BIBLIOGRAPHY

Hocho to Toishi. Tokyo: Shibata Shoten, 1999

Nozaki, Hiromitsu. *Meijin Itamae; Nihon Ryori no Hiden.* Tokyo: Kodansha, 2004

———. *Nihon Ryori no Kiso Gijuisu.* Tokyo: Shibata Shoten, 2004

———. *Waketokuyama Nozaki Hiromitsu no Karadani Ii Oishii Hanashi.* Tokyo: Bungenko, 2006

Naruse, Uhei, Nozaki, Hiromitsu, & Nishinomiya, Shinichi. *Zukai: Sakana no Sabaki kata.* Tokyo: Shibata Shoten, 1997

Kishimoto, Hirokazu, Suzuki, Nobuhiro, & Akagawa, Izumi. *Gyoruigaku Jikken Text.* Kanagawa: Tokai University Press, 2006.
(The illustrations on page 150 are based on those in this book.)

SELECTED KNIFE RETAILERS

Aritsugu Co., Ltd.
219, Kajiya-cho, Nishikikoji-dori Gokomachi-nishiiru, Nakagyo-ku, Kyoto-shi,
Kyoto, Japan
Phone: +81-75-231-1066   http://www.aritsugu.com

Hiyoshimaru Ltd.
Tokiwa Palace 516, 1-1-1, Shimo-ochiai, Shinjuku-ku, Tokyo, Japan
Phone: +81-3-3368-1598   http://www.houcho.net

Kai Corporation
3-9-5, Iwamoto-cho, Chiyoda-ku, Tokyo, Japan
Phone: +81-3-3866-3741   http://www.kai-group.com/e/

Kiya & Co., Ltd.
1-5-6, Nihonbashi-muromachi, Chuo-ku, Tokyo, Japan
Phone: +81-3-3241-1141   http://www.kiya-hamono.co.jp

Nenohi Co., Ltd.
Kaneshin Bldg. 1F, 4-10-5, Tsukiji, Chuo-ku, Tokyo, Japan
nenohi@nenohi.co.jp   http://www.nenohi.co.jp/

Tsukiji Masamoto Co., Ltd.
4-9-9, Tsukiji, Chuo-ku, Tokyo, Japan
Phone: +81-3-3541-8000   http://www.tukijimasamoto.co.jp/

INDEX